KU-537-860

GOD IS LOVE

J. W. Alexander

THE BANNER OF TRUTH TRUST

THE BANNER OF TRUTH TRUST
3 Murrayfield Road, Edinburgh EH 12 6EL
P.O. Box 621, Carlisle, Pennsylvania, 17013, U.S.A.

*

© Banner of Truth Trust 1985
First published as 'Sacramental Discourses' 1860
First Banner of Truth edition 1985
ISBN 0 85151 459 6

*

Reproduced, printed and bound in Great Britain by
Hazell Watson & Viney Limited,
Member of the BPCC Group,
Aylesbury, Bucks

THE lamented author of these discourses, in the preface to his last volume, writes: "Printing is only preaching in another shape. . . . After all, the controlling reason for publishing as well as preaching, should be a desire to glorify God in the salvation of men, by communicating, as widely as possible, the truth of the gospel." These discourses are selected from those preached to his people on Sacramental occasions, and as on such occasions he always presented topics connected with Christ and his atoning work, but little variety of subjects could be introduced.

Although these sermons were never intended or prepared for publication, yet I have not felt at liberty to change a single word, printing them just as they were written, which will account for the abruptness which appears in one or two instances; for example, in the last discourse, where it was found impossible to fill up the gaps in the introduction, and it was therefore omitted entirely.

In most of these instances there are indications of extemporaneous enlargement, which those accustomed to the unction and tenderness of the author's instructions at such seasons, might desire to see filled out; but alas, these overflowings of love for Christ and his people, these unwritten emotions which the presence of the cross and the sacrifice excited, all passed away with him.

May the prayers which accompanied the writing and preaching of these sermons, be now abundantly answered by that Immanuel whom they were intended to glorify.   S. D. A.

New-York, December 5, 1859.

CONTENTS.

I.

GOD IS LOVE.

GOD IS LOVE.

GOD IS LOVE.

1 John 4 : 8, 16.

"He that loveth not, knoweth not God; for God is love."
"And we have known and believed the love that God hath to us. God is love; and he that dwelleth in love dwelleth in God, and God in him."

If we can by Divine aid conduct our meditations aright on these words, we shall be led to such affection towards God, such tender remembrance of Christ, and such unfeigned communion with brethren, as shall adorn our sacramental feast. As the writer of our text clung more closely than any to the dying Redeemer, so his writings turn more than any on Jesus and his love. And in the following discourse, my proofs and illustrations shall be drawn chiefly from these writings.

The text brings us at once to a personal God; that object of love and worship, to whom we cling more firmly, the more he is denied. And alas that we should say it. He *is* denied. The day was when even the most fearful among us could not have apprehended that the form of horrid unbelief called pantheism could ever gain foothold in America. Yet we have lived to see it. No longer do we wrestle with the naked barbarism of Paine and Volney. The lowest class of foreign manufacturers in works and mills are beginning to consider that shape of infidelity to be obsolete. But another river of poison has begun to flow in from Germany, the nursing mother of all religious monsters. Instead of no God, it is all God. Instead of believing nothing, it is believing every thing. There is scarcely a term or phrase of orthodox and evangelical religion, which is not heard from the lips of those who but yesterday were dead rationalists, Unitarian scoffers, Priestleyan humanitarians. All systems are voted to have a form of truth. All heresiarchs from Cerinthus and Marcion, to Swedenborg and Joe Smith, are invested with a halo of pleasing attraction. The religion of Taste and Beauty, of Music and

Architecture, of Industry and Labor, has taken the place of the religion of Truth and Holiness. All worship has something good in it, whether addressed to Jesus, to Mary, to Jove or to Juggernaut. All we are and all we see, all that was is and shall be, is God. And God is a vast, mutable, fermenting, tumultuating, ever-developing ocean of universal being, an infinite impersonality which embosoms us and of which we are ourselves a part. Most clearly he who learns this must unlearn the God of the Bible. This is not the Jehovah of the Old Testament, nor God the Father of the New. Such a divinity as this, however hymned by the rhapsodies of fashionable poets, or glorified by a mystic philosophy, is not the God whom we can approach unto, and within whose almighty arms we can lie. Such a religion may answer for the mock battles of the schools, or the rhapsodies of verse, but it is too cold and intangible to sustain on the sick bed, or cast its guiding ray over the path into eternity; and indeed, we generally find those who maintain such views of God coupling with them a denial of personal distinct, that

is, individual existence beyond the grave.
Take away the keystone, and the arch
becomes ruinous. Very hard it is to unlearn
the errors of a false system, especially when
implicated with the phantasms of imagination; hence few come back, and most make
one plunge after another into hideous gulfs
of transcendental spiritualism, Swedenborgian
intoxication, and the licentious sweep of
what children of Gomorrah call passional
freedom. O my brethren, how gracious is
the hand (more than angelic) which leads
us back from the hell of such sulphureous
dreamings to the faith of our infancy: how
like emerging from a hot night in some
fever-hospital full of miasm and delirium
into the cool, clear morning air of mountains! How precious beyond all description the blessedness of approaching a personal God, who made us, who sees us who
hears us, who is near us who cares for us,
and who saves us. How heavenly the
declaration, "God is love."

To minds seeking to know who and
what God is—and this is the grand enigma
of the universe, which vexed the souls of the
greatest among the ancients—this declaration,

though imperfectly understood, must have been truly surprising and awakening. They spoke of the Supreme under various characters, but never had they dared to syllable his name as love. Never had any passion bearing such a title been directed towards him. When early inquirers, for example sad though learned Greeks, came to the ancient Scriptures, opened the scroll of this epistle, and read these words, twice occurring in this brief space, their emotions must have been novel. Let us examine the connexion in which the proposition occurs. In the first instance (4 : 8) the beloved disciple brings it forward in a manner which manifests the identity of love, in heaven and earth. "Beloved," he says, "let us love one another." This, you will say, is only the repetition of the familiar Christian maxim; all believers must love one another. But he adds, "Love is of God." Here he traces the flood to the fountain. In other words, love is divine, and proceeds from the very nature of God. And where holy love prevails, it is by reason of a new nature, from above, implanted by regeneration. For listen again: "Every one that loveth is

born of God and knoweth God." These
are most notable words, as showing us, that
true knowledge of God, which only the
regenerate possess, displays itself by love,
which thus is "of God." And further, stat-
ing the same negatively: "He that loveth
not, knoweth not God." The selfish, the
contracted, the malign, the unrenewed spirit
in man, has never beheld and known the
Supreme Excellence, "for God is love."
And not content with generalities, he cites
the great, the stupendous manifestation of
Divine love in the incarnation. (v. 9.) "In
this was manifested the love of God toward
us, because that God sent his only begotten
Son into the world, that we might live
through him." Propitiation proves love —
and love to sinners. Propitiatory love is
the chief outshining of the Supreme splen-
dor. This very principle (love) descends
from God to men, and shows us more of
God than all works and all symbols. There
is no direct vision of God; but there is
vision of love, when we see and love God's
image in a brother. Thus we may have
the indwelling of infinite love in our bosoms,
revealing much of God though we may not

gaze upon him with our eyes. (v. 12.) "No
man hath seen God at any time. If we
love one another, God dwelleth in us, and
his love is perfected in us." Through all
these verses (7–13) the golden thread of
connexion is the thought that love in God's
nature, love in atonement, love in Jesus, and
love in the brethren, are one and the same
holy principle. The second occurrence of
the text keeps up the same reference to the
cross as the sign of love. (v. 16.) True
faith owns God's infinite love in redemption,
admits the overflow of compassionate grace,
and thus unites God and the soul. "We
have known and believed the love that
God hath to us." Every sinner who receives
Christ can say this. God's smile is recognized. We no longer dwell under mere
justice and fear. We believe God to be
loving. Mark what follows: "God is love;
and he that dwelleth in love dwelleth in
God and God in him." (v. 16.) There is no
surer evidence of being united to God, and
therefore new-born, than the fact that we
dwell in love. It is our habitation; there
we live, never going out, or going out soon
to return; more—it is our atmosphere, in

which we live and move, and which we
breathe, with vital effects. This love is
awakened to life by God's love in redemption. The whole train of argument goes to
this, and we read all in the cross; (v. 19.)
"We love him, because he first loved us."
It was necessary, my dear brethren, that
we should see clearly how the apostle John
introduces the maxim, "GOD IS LOVE."

2. While every thoughtful mind that ever
heard this utterance has probably been struck
by a vague sublimity in the words, what, we
may still ask, are we to understand by them?
God is Love; but how, and in what sense?
Does it mean that God is loving, that he
loves, or that he is benevolent? This it
does mean, in a low and partial degree; this
is included; but this is far from the grandeur of the apostolic conception; and there
is immeasurable force in the abstract term.
Do the words intend, then, that Love or
Benevolence is so equivalent to God, as fully
to define God, so that all his glorious attributes are modes of this one attribute, and
so that there is nothing in God but love?
Some have so taught, and have resolved all
the divine perfections into love. Even jus-

tice and wrath, in their view are but varying aspects of this one excellency. As a
necessary accompaniment the same theologians have made all virtue or holiness to
consist in benevolence, and infinite holiness
in infinite benevolence. And some have
built this upon our text. But here we have
a striking instance of the evils which result
from an undue wish to simplify; or to refer
diverse effects to one and the same principle. Though benevolence is virtue, it is
not all virtue. Though all selfishness is sin,
all sin is not selfishness. Though God is
infinitely benevolent, infinite benevolence is
not all of God; who is infinite in being,
in truth, in power, and in eternal equity.
God is Love, and the maxim holds good
and abides glorious; but in the same sublime sense as God is Truth, and God is
Righteousness. The precise notion intended
to be conveyed, so far as human notions
can be precise respecting a divine object,
is this: that infinite love pertains to the very
nature and being of Jehovah, so that benevolence is ever present, ever abounding
and absolutely essential. Especially in that
side of his glory which is turned to us-

ward, or at that opening of the pillar of
cloud where the pillar of fire breaks forth
to our view, it is boundless love which we
behold. And as all we know clearly of our
Maker is through Grace, our knowledge of
the Supreme, by means of the plan of redemption, is principally a knowledge of him
as love. The entire connexion of the passage shows this to have been the Apostle
John's mind, (4: 9, 10, 14, 16.) God is love
in such wise, that when we sinners look up
to him through Christ we see nothing but
love, as he who looks up to the sun's flaming
disk in mid-heaven sees nothing but a blaze
of light. To us, as redeemed, God is love,
yea, all love; but we dare not assert that
there are in the Holy One no powers but
these, or no powers but those we know.
Such philosophizing were presumptuous and
profane, and is alluded to by me chiefly
because of certain errors of serious moment
which have flowed from it. Safer and wiser
is it, and certainly more delightful, to come
down from abstractions, to another and a
scriptural way of contemplating the God of
Love; and this is the point which is now
to occupy us.

3. Some great and good men have loved to dwell on the marks of divine goodness which are visible in the works of Creation and Providence; and for certain purposes of proof and illustration such surveys are highly valuable. Far, far be it from me, ever to join the counsels of those modern philosophers who despise the study of Natural Theology, and who think nothing is to be learned from the marks of design in Nature. Poor Voltaire, who though a Deist was no atheist, was not so blind but that he could say: "Newton believed in final causes; I also venture to believe in them; light is made for the eye, and the eye is made for light." Especially after we have the key placed in our hand by Scripture, we walk through the mighty halls of this universal palace with amazement and thankfulness rising at every step; our language being that of David, in the recurring refrain of Psalm 107: ("O Lord, how manifold are thy works; in wisdom hast thou made them all; the earth is full of thy riches.") "Oh! that men would praise the Lord for his goodness, and for his wonderful works to the children of men!" So

admitted, we find Nature and Providence
bearing the same relation to revelation, as
experiments and specimens do to a lecture
on science. But to the uninitiated ear of
Nature, Creation and Providence never tell
of love. All the wondrous works are dumb.
We might take some angel-guide, and voyage
from orb to orb, through all the stellar
paths, yet see no trace of mercy. As sinners we could catch no sigh of compassion
or promise of pardon. All these belong to
that innermost glory of the heart of God,
which is revealed by the Word.

4. But not only is it Revelation, my
brethren; it is revelation of Christ, which
teaches us that God is love. And though
this truth be not contained in the terms
of the text, it is fully expressed in the context, as we have seen. The point is important enough to bear repetition. (v. 8 and 9.)
" God is love; in this was manifested the
love of God toward us, because that God
sent his only begotten Son into the world,
that we might live through him." That
is to say; the manifestation to us, that God
is love, is in God's sending his Son. Here
is the principal shining forth of the hidden

glory of the Divine Nature. Here is the
central truth of Christianity. Here is that
on which faith fixes when it justifies the
sinner. He that lay on the bosom of Jesus
turns continually, just as an infant to its
mother's breast, to this truth, (v. 10.) "Herein is love; not that we loved God, but that
he loved us, and sent his Son to be the
propitiation for our sins." This takes us
one step onward: we read the infinite love
not merely in God's sending his Son, but in
his sending him to be a propitiation. It
is just here, that we perceive that (v. 11.)
"God *so* loved us." The way in which
propitiation demonstrates the greatness of
this love to us is this: we were objects
of punitive justice — we were already condemned—we could do nothing to save ourselves—none in the created universe could
save us — God Almighty could not save us
. . . at the expense of infinite right—
then, in that juncture, God interposed the
act which made salvation possible, the act
of propitiation. God is justice; but hear,
O heavens, God is love! (3 : 16.) "Hereby
perceive we the love of God, because he
laid down his life for us." There is a

moment in the experience of every true
believer, when he awakes, as out of a trou-
blous and distempered dream of wrath and
death and damnation, to the sweet, fresh,
childlike vision that Christ died for him,
and herein sees that God is Love. The
Cross speaks it. The faintly opening lips of
dying Jesus speak it. The language of the
eyes, O how much more eloquent than
words—of eyes swimming in death—speak
it. The blood that speaketh better things
than that of Abel, at five bleeding wounds
speaks it. O my brethren, it is propitiation, which tells, not only the love of the
Son but the love of the Father. Away
with the calumnious allegation of heretical
adversaries, denying the only Lord God who
bought them and putting them and him
to an open shame, as though we represented
God the Father as a bloodthirsty tyrant, to
be appeased only by the bloodshedding
of his more loving Son! God the Father
gives the Son; he devises the plan, and decrees the expiation. The immeasurable love
of the unseen Godhead is made visible to us
in the flesh of the Son. Long before the clos
ing scene Jesus himself uttered this to the yet

unsealed ears of that Pharisee and master of
Israel who stole to him by night: "For God
so loved the world, that he gave his only begotten Son, that whosoever believeth in him
might not perish, but have everlasting life."
(John 3 : 16, 17.) The benevolence compassion and grace which stream to us from the
Cross are waves that gush from the secret
fountain of paternal Deity, while the glory of
the Father shines on us in the face of Jesus
Christ. And thus it becomes more and more
apparent, as we study it more, that it is the
revelation of Christ which teaches us that
God is love.

5. While we were constrained to admit
that the contemplation of nature is insuffi-
cient to assure us of God's mercy and grace
to sinners, or fully to instruct us concerning
his benevolence, it is nevertheless true, that
after we have learnt these lessons at the cross,
and thus discovered the key to nature's hieroglyphic, we may return to survey the works
of infinite wisdom and power as the works of
him who is also infinite love. Then the prospect changes. It is no longer the same cold,
orphaned universe. "Old things are passed
away, behold all things are become new; and

all things are of God who hath reconciled us
to himself by Jesus Christ."

> "The common air, the earth, the skies,
>   To him are opening Paradise."

The pure vault of wintry heaven looks down
with its starry countenance all serenely radiant in love. The fragrance of forests and the
blush of summer flowers now come to us as
from a Redeemer. And every breath of
mercy in daily things is a whisper of grace,
from one who died for us.

6. It can never cease to be the capital
truth, through all stages of universal history,
in the progress of worlds, that God is love.
Heaven is the kingdom of God, and so the
kingdom of love. To go to heaven, is to go
to God, that is to sink into the bosom of
unfathomable love. This is the atmosphere
of the blessed. Born into this, the new creature begins to love. The pulses play from an
action at the heart of all, which is Jesus
Christ. Faith worketh by love. Believing
is immediately productive of loving. The
new affection is not yet ripe; but its nature
is determined forever. The love of the so
pardoned soul, is in the first instance a fervent

melting often passionate going-out of itself to Christ on the cross. The language of the true Church in all ages has been the same on this head. Every new convert understands our meaning here. For reasons already given, this love of Jesus, is love of God. Its action is mighty; impelling to unreserved submission and perfect obedience. "The love of Christ constraineth us." At this point we have the origin of evangelical obedience, which is not in order to obtain pardon, but the consequence of pardon. (5 : 3.) "For this is the love of God, that we keep his commandments; and his commandments are not grievous." Other marks of piety may be wanting or obscure, but the believer's love to the God of love; the response of love to love; the earthly echo to heavenly compassion, can never be absent. The soul can not utter the syllables, God is love, without experiencing the emotion. God in Christ is the object of your distinct personal affection, if you have been renewed by his spirit.

7. This statement of the influence which the doctrine has upon the soul, would be incomplete, if we did not add; it insures the love of brethren. We need not return upon

our track, to show that love is the same in all
its actings. JOHN, our teacher, reïterates the
lesson, that right feelings towards God will
produce right feelings towards man. " He
that saith he is in the light, and hateth his
brother, is in darkness even until now."
" We know that we have passed from death
unto life because we love the brethren."
And it is connected thus with the cross
(3:16.) " Hereby perceive we the love of
God, because he laid down his life for us;
and we ought also to lay down our lives for
the brethren." And this effect of a renewal,
which reinstates in us the image of God, is
traced up to its unfailing cause: (5:1.)
" Whosoever believeth that Jesus is the Messiah is born of God: and every one that loveth him that begat, loveth him also that is
begotten of him." Fellow-disciples are our
Father's children, and brethren of Jesus.
This is enough to secure fellowship. The
new nature, of love, flows interchangeably,
and constitutes communion.

8. Behold, my brethren, the holy stream
which circulates around the eucharistic
table; love in God to believers—love in
believers to God—love in brethren to bre-

thren; all comprised in the higher law, GOD IS LOVE. We are in the spot, of all others, where such affections may be best awakened and promoted; for we are at the cross. Here is the sacrifice of propitiation, in sacramental emblem. Here are the body and blood of Jesus, in visible commemoration. Here is the nearest view, vouchsafed to us this side of heaven, into the secret majesty of Divine perfection. Approach—but with reverence, for your hand is upon the vail, and within is the Holy of Holies. If it has insufferable splendors, it has also the Propitiatory above the ark. "Seeing then that we have a great high-priest, that is passed into the heavens, Jesus the son of God, let us hold fast our profession;" and "let us . . . come boldly unto the throne of grace, that we may obtain mercy and find grace to help in time of need."

II.

GOD'S GREAT LOVE TO US.

II

COUNT LUCANOR

GOD'S GREAT LOVE TO US.

ROMANS 8 : 32.

"HE that spared not his own Son, but delivered him up for us all, how shall he not with him also freely give us all things."

WITH how inadequate a comprehension do any of us read or hear this saying! To know its meaning, one would need to explore the eternity of the past, and the eternity of the future. For it tells of bounty having its spring in the counsels of ages, and of bounty which runs on, with branching abundance among immortal spirits in glory. Intermediate in this succession come all the good things of this life, which our Heavenly Father condescends to secure to us by promise. But the principal and absorbing object, set before the eye in this remarkable passage, is the most wonderful upon which any intellect could turn,

and yet—such is our privilege, even from infancy—the most familiar to our mind and
memory; namely, the love of God to sinful
man. Sometimes we are ready to wish it were
possible to travel backward on our line of
experience, to that point in childhood when
Gospel grace first came to our cognizance; or
else to stand in the position of some serious
inquiring heathen who opens his ear and heart
to the news of a redeeming God; that by
either of these ways we might get rid of the
dulness and indifference which our worn and
jaded souls derive from long hardening of
custom. My brethren, the freshness of apprehension and feeling which we desire can be
wrought in us only by faith; which the Spirit
of God produces by means of the Word. Continued attention to the one topic before us, may
be blessed to fit us for the enjoyment of ordinances. Devout consideration of the text will
cause it to yield us these two thoughts: *God's
love to us, in giving his Son; and God's love
to us, carrying with it, and certifying to the
soul, all subordinate blessings.* One points to
the cause, the other to the effects, and each
may be examined under a two-fold view,
which will give clearness to the discussion.

I. GOD'S LOVE TO US IN GIVING HIS SON
Here is a great and heavenly subject, which
may be properly considered under two aspects:
God's love to us is the blessing of blessings;
and is demonstrated by the greatest of gifts.

1. GOD'S LOVE TO US IS THE BLESSING OF
BLESSINGS. As we and all mankind are no
better than orphans in the universe if we have
no belief in a Divine Creator and Benefactor,
so even thus believing we must be miserable,
unless we are persuaded that he regards us
with favor. A Deity who is, or even may be,
maglignant towards us would inspire no feelings but those of slavish fear and sickening
horror, akin to the experience of heathen
devil-worshippers, who grovel in acts of propitiation to the powers they hate. Nor should
we derive any comfort or support from maintaining the existence of a Great Supreme, who,
as Epicurus dreamed, sat in the heavens indif-
ferent to human weal or woe. So soon as we
admit a Great First Cause, ever active in pre-
serving and governing all things, we begin to
feel an interest in his dispositions towards us;
and our inquiries become the more earnest and
yearning with every new apprehension of him
as infinite in wisdom and power. "How does

this glorious God regard me, and what may I reasonably expect at his hands?" These are questions which lie at the bottom of all religions, under every form of Theism. Study of Providence, in the obscure and awful volumes of history and experience, where the pages are often marked with tears and blood, does not ease the mind in regard to man's destiny, or that certainty which we would fain have for ourselves. That God governs and that he is just and ever good, is seen to be compatible with the existence of horrid miseries;—and what is to hinder these from being our own? What ensures us, that the next stage of existence may not be infernal? What shall make it undeniable, that as evils have been, so they shall not continue and increase? Dark doubtings like these, such as unassisted reason cannot exorcise, become of a blacker hue, when conscience tells us we are sinners, and when we behold vindicatory justice seeking amends of transgressors. Some voice therefore is hearkened for, which may credibly whisper that God is propitious. If He is our Enemy, we perish, and perish all the more because we cannot re-enter our original nothing. These boding thoughts, which belong to all

human beings, are those which predispose men
to seek for a revelation, and which when a
revelation is offered lead them to inquire wist-
fully at its oracle. Now the first teachings,
even of the Word of God, are not such as to
remove all doubt. The Law precedes the Gospel. Hope is smitten down, before it is lifted
to the rock of support. And when conscience
is thoroughly aroused, and sin makes its mo-
tions felt in the heart, the thought of the
Almighty One, clad in holiness and judgment,
becomes insufferable. Then it is, that he who
was previously careless as to his Creator, begins to comprehend that unless this glorious
Jehovah be his friend, it were better for soul
and body that he had never been born.
Deep thought, great knowledge, and just reasoning only add to these solicitudes; and the
more the light is thrown on the Scriptures
the more does the inquirer see that if God be
against him his misery is sure forever. These
are the conclusions at which many arrive, and
at which all would arrive, if guided by truth.
What would you offer a man, to take the
place of God's favor, or to neutralize his
wrath? Accumulate all honors, science, power, modes of delight or exaltation; and what

will they do for him, on whose soul and destiny the Lord God Omnipotent looks with a steady frown? Let us go further. . . Suppose it were possible for God to shower all other gifts on the earthly lot of man, yet withholding his love, . . would not this be mocking torture? On the other hand, give to any soul assurance of God's perpetual love, and you crown that soul with bliss. In cool, impartial moments, therefore, when reason is sound, all other good seems trifling compared with the love of the infinite Jehovah. The immortal creature needs nothing more to make it happy to all eternity. "There be many," cries David, "that say, who will show us any good? Lord, lift thou up the light of thy countenance upon us." Therefore we justly conclude that God's love to us is the indispensable favour, without which we have nothing; in other words, it is the blessing of blessings.

2. GOD'S LOVE IS DEMONSTRATED BY THE GREATEST OF GIFTS. The greatest gift is this: "He spared not his own Son, but delivered him up for us all." Other, lesser gifts there are, in gracious, yea, divine abundance, on which we might meditate; but all these

are branches from this one root, lesser loves
from this one love. We have seen the necessity under which fallen humanity lies, of
having some assuring utterance of God's
benevolence, to keep it from despair and
elevate it in blissful hope. The infinitely
benevolent Creator, who is also the Redeemer, chose to vouchsafe such a manifestation; but no human mind, probably no
finite spirit, could ever have had a suspi-
cion or conjecture, previously to revealing
inspiration, what shape this utterance would
take. When the mystery burst into revelation all heaven must have been struck
mute at so new, so awful a shining-forth of
the Divine majesty. The great method of
saving mankind may be looked at on various sides, from many points of observation, and in manifold relations, but we are
about to restrict our view to a single aspect of redeeming grace, namely, God's giving his Son. This will be enough, for it
reveals the heart of infinite compassion.
GOD IS LOVE; and the Divine fulness finds
no such fit outlet and effluence as in the
delivering up of the WORD for us all. The
due consideration of the act would carry

us back into the eternal ages of primeval
silence, when as yet no worlds had rolled
from the creative hand, when no angelic
spirit had gazed into the face of the First
Fair and First Good; when godhead as yet
was all, and the very relation of Creator
and creature lay hid in idea; when the
Word was with God, yea, "was God," co-
equal, consubstantial, coeternal.   But   we
must descend from, or rather assume, these
high points of theology, and fix our thoughts
on the simple truth, that " God spared not
his own Son."

The sonship with which we are familiar on earth is a copy or shadow
of that Eternal Sonship, existing between
God the Father and God the Son; and is
perhaps intended to enable us more ade-
quately to comprehend the grandeur and
tenderness of the gift.   When we read that
God spared not his " own Son ;" a number
of gushing affections, aptly furnish interpretation, as they spring in the parental heart.
Things heavenly take earthly types; and infinite throbbings of Divine love are translated into terms of domestic affection.   " The
Father loveth the Son," is a proposition true

in heaven as in earth; but the profundity, the loftiness, the amplitude of such love, neither men nor seraphs can comprehend, any more than they can circumnavigate and fathom infinity. Man was made in God's image, partly we conceive that he might have some notion of his spiritual Creator, and hence man's affections afford some key to the awful, inscrutable acts of the Divine Majesty. But these are so far above, out of our sight, that it is unspeakable relief, when by the incarnation we find the heart of God beating in a human bosom, and the pulses of infinite affection driving their stream through our own flesh. Yet behind all this is the infinite compassion on which the coming of Christ in human nature is founded. "In this was manifested the love of God toward us, because that God sent his only begotten Son into the world, that we might live through him." (1 John 4:9.) And here it is necessary to lift an obstacle out of the way, which artful enmity sometimes lays down, before the steps of ignorance. Our scheme of salvation by Christ is thus cavilled at by Deistical or Socinian unbelief: 'You make a mediator necessary, as though God were implacable. You make God a tyrant, thirsting for blood, and refusing to be appeased, but by the immolation of his more merciful Son.' This is a subtle and blasphemous mode of casting opprobium on the Scriptures and the cross; and with superficial thinkers and bigoted scoffers it finds too ready acceptance. The charge, whether it come from ignorance or malice, is purely false, and has its origin in the Father of Lies, who having failed to thwart Christ's work, now seeks to defame it. 'We do make a mediator necessary,' not however because God is implacable, but in order to carry out the benignant intentions of him who seeks how he may be a "just God," and yet "a Saviour." That we represent him as 'a tyrant thirsting for blood,' is a calumny which our souls abhor, and which we fling back to the pit from whose sulphureous smoke it came; for we honor HIM who desireth not the death of the sinner, and who waiteth to be gracious. Far from holding that our blessed God 'thirsteth for blood,' as these Sadducean slanderers allege; we gather out of the Scriptures every variety of tender

comparison to express the Divine earnest
ness to wrest the souls of men from imminent destruction. And when, by a profane
burlesque, our enemies stigmatize the God
whom we adore and love as, ' refusing to be
appeased save by the immolation of his
Son,' we reject the diabolic jeer with filial
indignation, and would gladly show them,
if enmity could allow them to hear reason,
that the tremendous sacrifice of Jesus was
the means originated by God himself for
the expression and manifestation of a love
to man which transcends all creature-con-
ception. Know ye, whose shallow theology
would pluck all that is mysterious and all
that is sublime from the system of salvation, that God gave his Son, and that in
so giving him, he affords the greatest possible manifestation of his uncaused love. In
other connexions, we might show, how other
perfections than love, made this sacrifice necessary to the declarative glory of God.

The passage before us is far from being
the only one, in which this form of the
great truth is set forth. The giving or delivering of the Son, is a favorite mode of
inspired expression. Those blessed lips had

not long been opened at the night-inter-
view with Nicodemus, before they uttered
this immortal sentence, since graven on a
million hearts: "For God *so* loved the
world that he gave his only begotten Son,
that whosoever believeth in him should
not perish, but have everlasting life."
(John 3 : 16.) The gift, according to the
Master, is a proof of love. And by a
change of figure, in the very next verse:
"For God sent not his Son, into the world
to condemn the world, but that the world
through him might be saved." The sending is, in God's intent, a means to salvation, and so a token of love. God "sent
his Son to be the propitiation." (1 John
4 : 10.) "The Father sent his Son, to be
the Saviour of the world." (1 John
4 : 14.) "Whom," says Paul (Rom. 3 : 25,)
"God set forth to be a propitiation." And
more strongly (2 Cor. 5 : 21 :) "For he
hath made him to be sin for us, who
knew no sin, that we might be made the
righteousness of God in him." And lest
opposers should say the sacrificial part was
wrested by wicked men out of God's hands,
in the exercise of their wicked freedom

against his design; we are taught that the
very murderers, guilty in the act, were
unconsciously causing the wrath of man
to praise God, and working out his decree.
For at Pentecost, Peter thus addresses
these executioners concerning Jesus: "Him,
being delivered by the determinate counsel and foreknowledge of God, ye have
taken, and by wicked hands have crucified and slain." (Acts 2 : 23.) In all
which places, the words "gave," "sent,"
"set forth," and "delivered," go to show
that the mediatorial work originated in
the will and purpose of God, and was
the demonstration of his love.

It is not merely a doctrine of Christianity;
it is the fundamental doctrine. There is no
Gospel without it. It is the very Gospel, or
glad-tidings. Every thing else in the Gospel
is but an expansion of this, God loves the
world of sinners. To preach "Christ and
him crucified," is to preach God's love.
The sinking wretch who believes in Jesus
and is saved, believes in God's love. All
the arguments by which we urge sinners
to credit God's willingness to receive them
run up into this: (1 John 4 : 10 :) "Here-

in is love, not that we loved God, but
that he loved us, and sent his Son to be
the propitiation for our sins." And this
therefore is what the convert to God feels
that he has attained—belief that God loves
him. Before, he had no knowledge of
God but as a legal Avenger. Even when
nearest to the kingdom, he was resting on
some supposed truth short of this, and
was all in darkness. Day broke, when he
looked up into the clear countenance of
God's love to him. The great efficacy of
the cross, indeed, towards God, is in the
way of expiation; but its great efficacy
towards us is as proof of love. Whatever
is wanting, this is always present in true
faith . . . persuasion of God's love in
Christ. And so, whenever we see the
things that are freely given us of God,
we recognize God's love as demonstrated
by the greatest of gifts.

II. GOD'S LOVE TO US, CARRYING WITH IT
AND CERTIFYING TO THE SOUL, ALL SUBOR-
DINATE BLESSINGS. That is to say, he that
so loved as not to spare his own Son, but
delivered him up for us all, cannot but with

him also freely give us all things. And this necessity of love, this certain out-flowing of streams from the fount, this plenitude of gratuitous kindnesses from the full heart of infinite grace, is made sure to the belief of the soul. Or, separately considered,

1. GOD'S LOVE CARRIES WITH IT ALL SUBORDINATE BLESSINGS, that is, all other blessings; because all other blessings are subordinated. This comprises all, as God comprises the universe. He who hath God hath all: he who hath God's love hath the world of Divine favors. The greater includes the less, or rather the whole includes the parts. God's love can not be conceived as greater, than when he gives his own Son, from his own bosom; gives him to be man, to be humbled, to be put to death, to bear punishment, to be made a curse. If a king were to give to his feeble bride, whom he had plucked with strong hand out of slavery, all his possessions, and a share of all his kingdom, surely she might rely on him for a piece of bread or a draught of water. This is just the argument of grace. God's great gift necessitates his lesser gifts. God's

own Son is so transcendent a donation —
how shall he not with him also freely give
us all things! The reason why some do
not enjoy the full force of this Divine logic,
is that they stagger about the premises. If
they only comprehended the immense value
of the original gift; if they could only catch
a glimpse of the glory, beauty, loveliness
and infinite dearness to the Father of him
who is in his bosom; if they did only follow him down from heaven to earth, through
his life, agony and bloody sweat, his cross
and passion, his burial, resurrection and ascension; if they only stood amazed, as well
they might, at this great love wherewith
God loved us, while we were yet dead in
sins;—why, brethren, they could no more
doubt God's love and willingness to bless,
in all things else, than the bride folded in
the embrace of affection can suspect the husband who has endowed her with his all,
of plotting her ruin. The entire unbroken
chain of covenant love hangs on God's intention, from the first link to the last; from decree to consummation. (v. 30.) "Whom
he did predestinate, them he also called:
and whom he called, them he also justified;

and whom he justified, them he also glorified." How natural, how irresistible the conclusion that immediately follows?   " What
shall we then say to these things ? If God
be for us, who can be against us ?" And
then our text: a text which embosoms all
the Gospel, in all its principle and all its
effects; source and flood; centre and circumference; love and bliss; from God to the
creature, for ever and for ever.

Seek no longer then Christian brethren, to separate the love of the Son
from the love of the Father. They
are but dimensions of one and the same
amazing orb. Seek rather, with all saints,
to comprehend what is the breadth and
length and depth and height, and to know
the love of Christ which passeth knowledge, that ye might be filled with all the
fulness of God. The reason why we do not
expatiate on the subordinate gifts, is that
they are innumerable; comprehending all
good which can tend to the happiness and
perfection of the creature. In the sublime
burst which follows our text, even the Paul-
ine diction reels under the load of benefit,
while his wide induction draws within its

circle, death, life, angels, things present, things to come, height, depth, yea, all creatures; tracing up all to the love of God which is in Christ Jesus our Lord." (v. 39.)

2. GOD'S LOVE TO US, CERTIFYING TO THE SOUL ALL SUBORDINATE BLESSINGS. Here doctrine turns into experience, as the bud becomes a flower. The doctrine was, God's love in the capital article leads by necessary result to his love in every other article: the experience is, I know and feel it to be so; I open my heart to the greater good and to those which are less; I believe and am persuaded, that God is for me, and that none—that nothing can be against me. If this is wanting in any of us, it is because we have not faith. And here, my brethren, I am bound to testify, whomsoever it may startle or offend, that a large number of Christians, even in those which they consider their most profitable moments, go about the work of obtaining peace in their hearts by an inverted process; the very opposite of what is prescribed in the New Testament. When doubts overcloud their confidence, when remaining sin stirs inwardly, when the future looks portentous, when

their religion has become all trembling and
tears — what is it they do? Perhaps you
know this very sacramental hour. They sit
down to the work of exclusively scanning
and measuring wretched, imperfect self. They
turn over the massive books, filled with their
own liabilities. They debit themselves with
ten thousand items which they can never pay.
They hope by this method to find a balance
so favorable that they shall be able to rise
hoping in God, and therefore to apply to
promises made to regenerate persons. I
dare boldly pronounce, from God's word,
that genuine evangelical comfort was never
produced in this way; never, never, never.
This Sinai never yet uttered peace, while
it has thundered many a believer into
temporary despair. What then is the
right way? We need attention, for we
are touching the very vital point of difference between old divinity and the new,
between the joyful free grace which from
the silver trumpets of Luther, Melancthon,
Calvin, Knox and Cranmer, shook and
melted Europe in a great portion of its
Church--and that substitute of alleged im-
provement but real retrocession to Popish

legalism, which has made the chief part
of many experiences to consist in doubting, and which, if pursued to legitimate
results, would speedily land us in a scheme
of self-salvation. It ought to be clear to
any reason, that the ground of a sinner's
trust in Christ for salvation must be something independent of, and prior to, any
exercises of his own soul; yea something that is the cause of such exercises;
and therefore, that when doubts arise, the
resort to ultimate support, must be to this
same pre-existing and Divine ground. And
what can this be, but the Divine veracity,
assuring us that God loves us! Precisely
for this reason is Faith so often dwelt on
as the instrument; because faith, as faith,
lays hold of God's veracity; and trust is
nothing else but faith in a promise. Here
then is our experience of God's love, when
" the love of God is shed abroad in the
heart by the Holy Ghost;" and here the
way of direct escape out of Satan's legal
net. Poor pilgrim, hast thou like Bun-
yan's mythic Christian been confronted by
Moses and left smarting? — flee to Jesus
Christ. All Martin Luther's experience was

a wrestling against the demon of legality. God was preparing him to teach a free gospel with a strength of expression which makes his book on the Galatians, a golden volume. "But thou wilt say, (says he, on Gal. v. 5,) "I feel not myself to have any righteousness, or at the least, I feel but very little. Thou must not feel, but believe that thou hast righteousness. And except thou believe that thou art righteous, thou dost great injury unto Christ, who hath cleansed thee by the washing of water through the Word, who also died upon the cross, condemned sin, and killed death, that through him thou mightest obtain righteousness and everlasting life." O how precious to my recollection is St. Mary's Church Aldermanbury, near which I once lodged, because there it was that Poor Joseph having a large parcel of yarn hanging over his shoulders, went in and heard the text which saved him. 1 Tim. 1 : 15. On his dying bed, the happy, simple soul possessed the certitude of God's love to him as a sinner. For (you remember) when some of the religious sort asked 'But what say you of

your own heart, Joseph? Is there no
token of good about it? no saving change
there? Have you closed with Christ, by
acting faith upon him?'—'Ah no!' replied he 'Joseph can act nothing—Joseph has nothing to say of himself but
that he is the chief of sinners; yet seeing
that it is a faithful saying that Jesus, he
who made all things, came into the world
to save sinners, why may not Joseph after
all be saved?"—We have stood by the
dying bed of great and learned Christians, long the guides of others in theology;
but their faith was that of Poor Joseph;
a divinely-wrought persuasion of God's
love to them, evidenced by the gift of
his own Son. The nearest, safest, truest
way to Christ, is the direct way. After
all your self-examinations, preparations and
conditions, you will have to throw them
away, and come thus at last. Come now;
—and from the opened side behold all blessings issuing in a perpetual, widening, deep-
ening river. What is it that can harm
you, if you accept of God's own Son?
Condemnation? "it is God that justifieth."
Death for your sins? "it is Christ that

died, yea rather that is risen again, who is even at the right hand of God, who also maketh intercession for us." Can he condemn or punish?—such is the meaning—he, who died, who rose, who reigns, who intercedes! Look to HIM, and away with self and all deservings. And if you fear your own weakness, lest you should fall away, know that security against this also is in the grant. Because it were nugatory and dishonorable to the Scriptures, so to interpret 35–39 as if they meant that though "tribulation, distress, persecution, etc.," though "angels, principalities, powers," etc., cannot separate us from Christ, yet that sin can and may! Shocking nullification of the covenant! For how could any or all of these ever separate except by sin! And what a glorying would that be or appear to be, if all he meant was, "Thank God, I shall never be separated, unless I sin, and so separate myself!" No, dear fellow-believers, ye have not so learned Christ, nor has this been the hope you have derived from his word when you have heard him say: "I give unto them ETERNAL LIFE; and they shall never perish, neither shall

any man pluck them out of my hand."
1 J. 10 : 28. Feeble would be the reliance, if eventual salvation hung suspended
on the hair of our own will, which might
break under Satanic temptations in the
last hour! But no! "I am persuaded
that neither death, nor life, nor angels, nor
principalities, nor powers, nor things · present nor things to come, nor height, nor
depth, nor any other creature, shall be
able to separate us from the LOVE OF
GOD, which is in Christ Jesus our Lord."

'The Love of God' — it is our theme.
We have seen it comprehending and certifying all, through the gift of the Son.
And hence it is, that you have this
morning heard so little of merely temporal benefits. Christ gives these indeed,
out of his immeasurable fulness, but gives
them only as appendages to the chief
good. "God will give grace and glory;
no good thing will he withhold from them
that walk uprightly." Have you, the
greater gift, my suffering brother or sister?
be assured you shall have the less.
Whatever is best for your ultimate blessedness and glory, will be dispensed to you,
in due manner, measure and time. The

unreconciled hear this with disgust. A Gospel which should offer earthly good, is all the Gospel they desire; and if they sometimes faintly sigh for religion, it is in hope of increasing selfish earthly good. But you, who have been taught by the Spirit to consider sin the grand evil, and Christ the all-comprising good, you will rejoice in this gradation of benefits . . . first my Saviour, then his gifts. For you have learnt to look at the things which are not seen, but are eternal. And experience has long since convinced you, that you never had so much real enjoyment of worldly things, as when you forgot them entirely, as a distinct object of pursuit; and that you never really knew what happiness in religion was, until you made an entire, unreserved surrender; relinquishing to the world, and to worldly communicants, the race after riches, the contest for place, the miserable rivalry of lineage, dress, equipage, entertainment and expense, the pride of knowledge, art and literature, and girded up your loins to await the Lord's coming.

III.

THE TWO NATURES OF CHRIST.

THE TWO NATURES OF CHRIST.

Rom. 9 : 5.

"Whose are the fathers and of whom, as concerning the flesh, Christ came; who is over all God blessed for ever. Amen."

WE are sometimes challenged by Unitarians to produce any text, in which Christ is distinctly said to be God. Here is just such a text. *Christ is God over all blessed for ever.* The words bear no other meaning. You may deny that they are in the book, or you may deny that the book is true and authoritative; but once receive this New Testament, and you are constrained to the profession, *Christ is God.* Human language cannot be plainer. Sit down and imagine a phrase which shall most unequivocally and unanswerably tear up Socinianism by the roots, and you can invent nothing more to the point than this.

The more you look at it in its connexion
and examine all its parts, the more will it
stand out as a prominent and undeniable
assertion of the godhead of Jesus.   No
one could ever have dreamed of putting
any other signification on the words, if there
had not been something repulsive to proud
human intellect in the truth declared.   The
words are plain enough: the doctrine
taught in them is mysterious.   And haughty
worms spurn mysteries.   They are unwilling
that God should reveal any thing which
they could not have discovered themselves.
They can not consent that there should be
any recesses in the Divine nature which
they have not explored.   They marvel that
God should be greater than man.   To such
God might say, as to Job, out of the whirl-
wind, Job 38 : 4   " Where wast thou, when I
laid the foundations of the earth ? declare,
if thou hast understanding."   Or, in the
famous words of Agur, Prov. 30: 4   " Who
hath ascended up into heaven, or descend-
ed ?   Who hath gathered the wind in his
fists ?   Who hath bound the waters in a
garment ?   Who hath established all the
ends of the earth ?   What is his name,

and what is his son's name, if thou canst tell?" — We might remind them, that it was said of Messiah, in prophetic days, Isa. 9 : 6 His name shall be called Wonderful, Counsellor, the Mighty God, the Father of Eternity." All this would weigh little with persons who come to God's revelation with a ready-made creed, a product of their own understanding, fully made up as to what they are to find in the Bible, before they approach it. But for this determination no one would ever have found any obscurity in the text. Read it again, and observe how you are shut up to one meaning. Paul is speaking of the Jewish nation 1-4 "*whose*," says he, "are the fathers, and of whom, as concerning the flesh, Christ came, who is over all God blessed for ever." "*Who* is over all:"—there is no antecedent to this relative, but "Christ." Christ, undeniably, is over all God blessed forever. Nor can our adversaries evade this, till they have tortured the whole passage; put a full stop after "Christ;" and made a new sentence, thus, "God is over all blessed for ever." Extraordinary presumption! Amazing abruptness of transition! Compare the sentence thus produced, in order to get rid of _the divinity of Christ; mark how it hangs together, "Of whom, as concerning the flesh, Christ came. God is blessed for ever. Amen." For such a change there is no authority.

Examine the verse in its connexion (for half our expository blunders arise from tearing single sentences out of their connexion) and you will perceive that as soon as Paul begins here to speak of Christ, he speaks of him under a twofold character. Observe—"Of whom, as concerning the flesh . . . that is, 'of whom, as concerning the human nature,' Christ came. Now, I put it to every impartial reader, does not this prepare for some corresponding clause? Does not the mind irresistibly run on, and wait for something more? saying to itself, Christ, as concerning the flesh, came of the Israelites; but what does the Apostle go on to say Christ came of as concerning his higher nature? The common reading supplies this, and no other reading does, to our entire satisfaction. "Of whom (Israelites) as concerning the flesh, Christ came," in his inferior nature; and if you crave to know of whom he came as concerning his superior nature, then know ye that he "is *over all God blessed* for ever."

No wonder, my brethren, that all who wish to degrade the character of the Redeemer, labor to pervert this passage. If ingenuity and zeal could have changed its meaning, this would have been accomplished. But all arts have failed. There it stands. A resort to various readings and other copies has effected nothing. All ancient copies and manuscripts agree in giving the words just as we have them. They perfectly agree with the whole drift of the argument. It was the very object of the Apostle in these verses to exalt the Jewish nation as much as possible, and nothing was more natural than for him to declare the dignity conferred on them, by the fact, that, according to his human nature, he was an Israelite, who, in another nature, was God over all, blessed for ever. The words thus understood perfectly agree with other passages of Sacred Scripture. Let one suffice—from this very epistle. 1 : 3, 4. He designates the Gospel of God, as "concerning his Son Jesus Christ our Lord, who was made of

the seed of David according to the flesh
(observe how parallel with our text); and
declared to be the Son of God with power,
according to the Spirit of holiness ;" that
is, according to the divine nature.   Here
we have the very same antithesis or contrast as in the text; first the human nature, secondly the divine nature.

After this explanation of what the
words mean, we are prepared to assert, on
authority of inspiration, that CHRIST JESUS
THE LORD HAS TWO NATURES. This is denied by all Socinians and others, who
maintain that the Lord Jesus was a mere
man; only differing from others in this,
that he was the best of prophets and the
best of men.   They admit only a single
nature, and scout the idea of two natures
in one person; a union which their amazing
advancement into the wonders of the Divine nature authorizes them to declare absurd and impossible.

The doctrine of Christ's two natures
likewise met with opposition from another
quarter, that is to say from some who admitted the divinity of our Lord. A noted
teacher and leader, Eutyches by name, lived

at Constantinople, in the fifth century. In striving to combat Nestorius and others, who separated the human and the divine so as to make two persons, Eutyches sought to deny two natures. He readily admitted that there were originally two natures, that the Godhead and the humanity had been distinct; but that upon the incarnation the two became one.* Thus the human nature was by him turned into the divine. The lower was absorbed into the higher: to use their own expression the human was swallowed up in the Divine. There is no ground for this in the Scriptures. It is not said that the flesh was made the Word, but that the Word was made flesh. Throughout the Gospel account we find both natures remaining, in mysterious union, yet perfectly distinct. The Lord Jesus Christ, "being the eternal Son of God, of one substance and equal with the Father, in the fulness of time became man, and so was, and continueth to be, God and man, in two entire distinct natures, and one person forever." This is the clear New Testa-

* Pearson on the Creed, Art. 3. p. 246.

ment account. (Gal. 4 : 4.) " God sent forth
his Son *made of a woman.*" Yet the miraculous conception and birth resulted in
more than man; it was more than a mere
man produced by divine miraculous power.
(Luke 1 : 35.) "That holy thing which
shall be born of thee, shall be called the
Son of God." The infant Saviour was at
once Son of Mary and Son of God. And
in his humanity was divine perfection in-
corporated: "for in him dwelleth all the
fulness of the Godhead bodily." Col. 2 :
9. This is by no means a theological
nicety. There are times in every ripe experience when we taste the sweetness of
recognizing our Redeemer in each of his
natures. We behold them blended and yet
not in confusion. Did he cease to be man,
we should miss that chief tie, which binds
us to divinity—that chief source of sympa-
thetic confidence—and that chief glory of
our nature. Did he cease to be God, we
should feel ourselves thrown back in the
matter of salvation on the resources of
bare human nature, the strength of a great
prophet and martyr. There could be no
bringing together, as now, of the divine

and the human. And on the other hand, this divinity and this humanity, equally distinct objects of our vision, and equally precious to our faith, exist in one Christ, sole and undivided; one glorious Person, whose name is Wonderful, and whose like is not in the universe. This has been the doctrine of the Catholic Church for hundreds of years. Heretics and errorists have gone off on one hand and on the other, but the great body of universal Christendom has held the same established path. Nor was this one of the matters in regard to which our fathers made their protest at the time of the Reformation. The Church even of Rome was sound in regard to the two natures of Christ. The Council of Trent and the Confession of Augsburg here speak the same language. We have no quarrel at this point with even popish tenets. The place where reformed theology diverged, where the dominant Church had wandered from apostolic teaching, and where we have returned to it, is in the doctrines of grace and justification—the fall of man and his recovery. But as to the triune God and the preexistence of Christ, the true and Scriptural doctrine was enounced, settled, and put beyond dispute, before the great schism, a division between the East and West. Hence nothing can be more exact or discriminating more full and satisfactory than the ancient creeds in the Greek language. And the doctrine of two natures in one Christ is clearly made known in the words of our text.

I. It declares that CHRIST OUR MEDIATOR IS GOD. There are reasons for this stupendous truth which, I suppose, neither men nor angels can penetrate: but there are other reasons which are things revealed, and, as such, belong to us and to our children. (1.) It pleased God to accomplish our salvation by an intensity of suffering. That this was necessary, we may be sure; as God could not otherwise consent to bruise his only begotten Son. Suffering, be it observed, was an indispensable element in the atoning world. No created pencil could depict, no human eloquence or tongues of angels describe, what passed in the soul of the Redeemer at Gethsemane and Calvary. Suffering, raised to agony, and transcending human endurance, was the price of our pardon. The Lord took flesh for this very purpose, that he might be a sufferer. The degree of this suffering was beyond all human strength to bear. Man could have borne much under uncommon supports of grace; but the utmost so endured would have fallen short of atoning for a single additional soul: what shall we say of atoning for millions; of atonement ample for a world!

The wrath of God is not an unmeaning term: it was due to us; it was borne by Jesus. To bear it required the sustentation of the divine nature. The penalty of the law was death; not merely the pang of dissolution, but that heavier death which finite beings could not have exhausted in an eternity. Christ tasted of this death. God raised him up, "having loosed the pains of death; because it was not possible that he should be holden by it." The Divine nature bore up the human under unparalleled and awful sufferings, but for which support it would have sunk and perished. The universe beheld the glorious sight, of one like ourselves, and under our yoke, made strong to suffer, and opening a boundless capacity for the reception of pains, before which simple humanity would have vanished in a moment. The divine nature in Christ was necessary, that the human nature might endure the shock.

2. The threefold functions of our Lord, in suffering for us, obeying for us, and interceding for us, are all dependent on his personal merit. The value of suffering is in the dignity of the sufferer. The value of obedience is in the dignity of him who obeys. And the prevalence of intercession depends on the influence and glory of the intercessor. In each of these three offices the power of a mere man would reach but a little way. His pangs were next to useless, at best but martyrdom. His obedience were no more than payment of his own debt. And his prayers for others at the court of heaven might prove as inefficacious as those of Jeremiah or of Job or of Samuel. But add divinity, that is infinitude — and how does the mediatorial work tower above all reach of computation! Now we see why the Messiah must be God. The divine nature becomes the golden altar, on which

the human body and soul of Jesus is laid,
a spotless victim: and the "altar sanctifieth
the gift." The obedience to law of the
Son of God, born of a woman, made under
the law, is such as honours that law more
than all angelic rectitude could do, and
becomes such a righteousness as that by it
"many may be made righteous." And in
the heavenly court what can resist the
pleadings of God's well beloved Son; whom
the Father heareth alway? Such dignity
is conferred upon all these parts of the
mediatorial work, that even those which are
primarily transacted in the human nature,
as all suffering and all obedience must be,
are nevertheless regarded as divine, by reason of the intimate union of the divine
and human natures. The Scriptures attribute to one what in strictness of speech
belongs only to the other. Thus we are
taught Acts 20. 28 "to feed the. church
of God, which he hath purchased with his
own blood." And on the other hand the
Son of Man John 3 : 13, is said to be
then in heaven. Indeed it is so evident
that divinity is necessary to propitiation and
vicarious obedience, that as soon as a man

gives up the proper divinity of Christ, he
gives up the atonement. Or, to speak more
properly, when he has given up the atonement, he sees that he has abandoned all
that made a divine nature necessary in
Messiah, and so he denies any such divine
nature. This is the pedigree of Unitarian-
ism. The first step in this series of errors
is the rejection of substitution, and of a
properly penal character in the sufferings
of Christ. By a natural process this leads
down to the gulf of Socinian unbelief. If
the Mediator had not been God, there
would have been no efficacy in his mediatorial work.

3. The satisfaction of divine Justice
which is involved in every just notion of
Atonement, demands something more than
man. The wound inflicted by sin, on God's
declarative glory, was too deep to be
healed by the holy life or temporary pain
of the best of men, even though he were
immaculate. There are teachers abroad,
brethren, who will tell you, that there is
no such satisfaction; that it was no part
of Christ's errand; and that in regard to
pardoned sinners God's justice is never sat-

isfied. Pardon is therefore an act of absolute divine sovereignty; and might as well, so far as appears, have followed the oblation of a lamb, as the oblation of Christ. According to our view, the oblation of Christ was necessary, because justice had been so signally insulted, that no reparation could be sufficient, but that which offered the covenanted humiliation of an infinite person; and to render this, God became man. 4 In carrying out the same glorious purpose, the Redeemer procures God's favour for his people, in his divine character, as Son of God; "to the praise of the glory of his grace, &c." He carries this point with a vehemence of triumphant authority and resistless right. 5 So also he arose from the struggle of his human sufferings as the Head of a countless retinue, all ransomed by his arm and bought to be his followers; inasmuch as "he gave himself for us, that he might redeem us from all iniquity, and purify unto himself a people, zealous of good works." Nor is he content with leading them; he reigns over them, subdues and holds in check all their enemies, and abides their everlasting

Head.   Sending down upon them by promise that Holy Spirit of God, whom we cannot for a moment conceive to be at the bidding of a glorified man, however exalted.   In all these particulars we clearly perceive how truly it was requisite that the Mediator should be *very God.*

II. The text declares that CHRIST OUR MEDIATOR IS MAN : " Of whom, as concerning the flesh, Christ came." It is unnecessary to prove that the word " flesh " in this passage is not taken in any one of those several New Testament acceptations, which involve the conception of sin. " In him was no sin." Neither does it mean the human body alone ; as if the Divine Nature had merely assumed a body, and been the sole animating principle of this body, without any human spirit. The Son of God took to himself a true body and a reasonable soul. We seldom meet in our day, with any followers of those ancient heretics,* who denied the existence of a human soul in Christ. The tendency of the age is too much away from the spiritual and the

* Apollinarists, Bretschneider, § 98.

mystical to favour this class of errors: the opposite class is rife—those I mean which grow out of rationalism, which sink the divinity, and represent our Mediator as man and only man. Nevertheless we must not allow extremes on this side to drive us from the important and indispensable work of holding forth the Lord's humanity. He is true and proper man, having taken the nature not of angels, but of the seed of Abraham. In this sense Paul declares him to have come of Israel "according to the flesh." The phrase is delightfully illustrated by 1 Tim. 3:16: "Great is the mystery of godliness: God was manifest in the flesh . . . . seen of angels:" as if even angels could see God only by means of incarnation. Again, "God sent his Son in the likeness of sinful flesh." In Peter's sermon at Pentecost Acts 2:30 he quotes David of whom he says, "Being a prophet, and knowing that God had sworn with an oath to him, that of the fruit of his loins according to the flesh—he would raise up Messiah to sit on his throne." How unmeaning would such words be ('according to the flesh') if Messiah was to exist according to no other nature! But our present use of them is to illustrate the text, and affirm the human nature of Messiah. "The Word was made flesh and dwelt among us." Confident of your belief of this august doctrine, permit me to give a few reasons why it was requisite that our Mediator should be Man. 1 Great is the advantage my brethren of holding fast to the representative principle in religion. It is a key that opens many theological locks. All that Christ does as Mediator he does representatively. He acts as a public person. He transacts for many. This led him to become man. It is far too low a view of the subject to think of Christ as standing off at a distance and conferring benefits on man. No; in order to transact on man's behalf, he becomes man. In this nature he makes the awful plunge into abysses of degradation and pain: in this nature he emerges, ascends and carries up our manhood in a glorious exaltation. The human nature sits in Christ Jesus on an eminence which could never have been reached, but by the incarnation. Christ must needs become man, if he would exalt man's nature. 2 In the progress of this unparalleled representative work, it was necessary that obedience should be rendered to Law. Here you have a second reason for the manhood of Christ. As God he could not be amenable—he could not obey. As a person, combining godhead and humanity, he could, and did, hold himself subject to the legal demands. "By the obedience of one shall many be made righteous." This active righteousness was accomplished by Christ, standing at the head of the vast column of believers, and for them; and consists in the totality of his holy principles, thoughts, feelings, purposes, words, works, and abstinences from evil.

3 But our thoughts become still more solemn when we consider the grand essential part of the Atonement, that is, the suffering of Christ. It was necessary that he should suffer; and yet except in humanity he could not suffer. Strictly speaking, God can no more suffer, than he can cease to exist. If in certain passages he is said to suffer, and to die, it is so said

only in the same sense in which he is
said to shed his blood. God (need I say
it) has no blood, except the blood of his
assumed humanity, and God in like manner has no suffering, but the suffering of
his assumed humanity. This humanity
was assumed for the very reason that
there could be no suffering without it.
But when the humanity is assumed, and
God and man united in one Person, theology attributes to the undivided person
the acts and attributes of either nature;
nay, even attributes to one nature the acts
and attributes of the other nature. *Com-
municatio idiomatum.* Hence we explain
all expressions which ascribe suffering to
Jehovah, who would cease to be Jehovah,
the moment he ceased to be happy. "For-
asmuch then as the children are partakers
of flesh and blood, he also himself likewise took part of the same; that through
death he might destroy him that had the
power of death." For all the common
purposes of daily Christian experience we
need no nice discriminations. Let us fix
our eyes and hearts on the One adorable
Person, CHRIST, suffering and dying for us.

4 Another reason is the ground afforded for the affectionate confidence of Christ's people, in troubles and temptations. He is Man, therefore he can feel with us! Who has not admitted it a hundred times! Sweet is his human name, JESUS! There are moments when it is the sweetest of his names: and when among his "many crowns" the loveliest is his human crown of thorns. As God, he could indeed approach us, but how could we approach him? This is the very door to the inner sanctuary. "For we have not a High Priest which cannot be touched with the feeling of our infirmities; but was in all points tempted like as we are, yet without sin." That 'holy thing' which came of Israel, was our flesh and blood. He too was born of woman; he too was wearied, was wasted, was in tears and blood, was in temptation and death. In our hour of anguish it is of infinite consolation to resort to Christ's wounded humanity, and to bear our sufferings under the recollection that he has borne the same.

5 The result of all these considera-

tions is that Christ is not only a Lord and
Saviour, but "according to the flesh" an
Elder Brother; and by this connexion we
"receive the adoption of sons:" if sons,
heirs of God and joint heirs with Christ.
Our language is his language, namely,
Abba, Father! The throne of God becomes the throne of grace, when we behold there, seated in benignant power, one
who is very man as well as very God.
And our religious experience is incomplete,
if we do not perpetually refresh our
thoughts with views of the Lord Jesus
Christ as a man.

III. But, as was said before, while
we contemplate the divine nature and
the human nature, as unconfused, and
eternally distinct, we must equally contemplate the Lord our Saviour as one
Christ, uniting both natures in One Person. There is a divine fitness and beauty
in this. Not only are we kept from being
distracted in our thoughts first in one direction and then in another, but we find
a relief in knowing that here is a "Daysman betwixt us," Job 9 : 33, that may

"lay his hand upon both." The great work was to reconcile God and man: here is a glorious Person who is both God and man. GOD so looks on the undivided Person. God accepts the work belonging to each nature, as the work of the whole person — as the work not so much of God — or of man — as of Christ, at once God and man. We also should so look on the undivided Person; we should by faith behold and receive and trust in the works of each nature, as the works of one adorable Christ. I conceive it to be important to counsel all believers, and especially those who are young and simple-hearted, to beware of perplexing their minds with the high points pertaining to this subject. LOOK AT CHRIST. There fix the eyes of your mind. Be not overmuch anxious to discern what belongs to one nature, and what to the other. Fix your contemplation on his Person. Behold him dying, behold him reigning. There is no danger of going astray, when in your common thoughts and prayers, your whole soul goes forth to a single undivided object — Christ.

Are you feeling for his support, and resting on his sympathies, as a man: you do well—he is bone of your bone and flesh of your flesh. Are you praying to him, as God. You do well — you do no more than dying Stephen, who said "Lord Jesus receive my Spirit:" for he is God over all, blessed for ever!—If you wish to have the grand secret of religion couched in a single maxim; if you would learn how to be reconciled and how to abide so; if you would be strengthened against temptation, if you would be holy and happy, take this rule: LOOK TO CHRIST! Just so much piety have you, as you have Christ in your thoughts. Lay it before your minds as the great Christian lesson of your lives, to study the person of Christ. Make it your delightful task, to become more and more acquainted with it. As you would diligently traverse a great domain, every part of which you were bound to know —so set yourself to expatiate over the character and personality of Jesus Christ as recorded in the Scriptures. Begin the New Testament and never stop reading it over and over, with this very thing in view, to learn more and more of the Lord. His own light will shine on his own glorious countenance, and as you read again and again, you will see its lineaments radiant with higher and higher illumination; each adorable feature will be more distinct and familiar; you will know it better; as the face of a friend of a brother of a CHRIST (for all other words come short); you will feel the fleshly tablet of your heart receiving the rays from this 'Shining in the face of Jesus;' and as you feel the reflection of this Sun of righteousness, you will own an unwonted glow; beholding as in a mirror the glory of the Lord you will be changed into the same image. The work of inward assimilation is going on. As you hold the soul, by loving contemplation, in these beams, the pencil of heavenly light is drawing Christ's image within you. The table of the heart is becoming his best and most cherished portrait. Desist not then from such study of his person as shall cause you, day by day, to be more reflective of his image.

It follows from this, that I consider the

deliberate and perpetually increasing study of Christ's person, in the New Testament, as the principal means of grace. *If you know Christ, you know every thing.* Here there can be no excess. You cannot by possibility, visit him too often, or love him too much. This daily endeavour to fix your heart on the person of Christ, God and man, will regulate all your other experience. Never fear lest it make you a one-sided Christian. It is the very means of symmetry. Because it is looking at the central-point of the painting. All other truths, as subordinate, will fall, of themselves, into their true relation. Open your bible every day, with the inquiry, What more can I this day learn of Christ? Try to live over the scenes of the type-prophecy of gospel history, with the eye always on him whom you love. Begin in Eternity. Proceed to Bethlehem—to Egypt—to Nazareth—to the Temple. Follow him, increasing in stature and in favor both with God and man. Mingle with the throng, and approach him, on the crowded highways, beside the lake, at Jordan, at the feasts. Join yourself to a more favored few, and penetrate to his miracles, to his sermons, to his transfiguration, to his paschal supper, to his passion, resurrection and ascension. Follow him upwards, and remember him as " Jesus Christ, the same yesterday to day and forever." As you do this; as you dwell on his peculiar traits; as you gain light on mysteries; as you perceive at one time his humanity, and at another time his godhead, most prominent; you will be disposed with Paul to add your loud response, to the declaration of the text, " Of whom as concerning the flesh- Christ came who is over all God blessed forever." I say you will from a full heart add AMEN!

IV.

THE HYMN OF THE EUCHARIST.

THE HYMN OF THE EUCHARIST.

MATT. 26 : 30.

"AND when they had sung an hymn, they went out into the Mount of Olives."

IN some respects this is one of the most remarkable statements in the life of our Saviour. We have seen him in various conditions and circumstances, in prayer, in teaching, in frequent suffering and once in joy, but never before in the exercise of vocal praise. Yet there can be no doubt that he took his part with devout Israelites in the songs of the temple-service, and we may readily imagine that as well in the social group of disciples, as in the more sacred devotions of the private hour, his pure and lofty affections found vent in holy psalmody, of which this is the appropriate and sometimes the only

adequate utterance. In following the series
of events in our Lord's earthly history, we
have followed him to the very eve of his
great suffering. We have sat with him at
his sacramental table, and listened to those
simple, touching and profound discourses,
which he spake in that hour of wistful
expectation. But now the little assembly
is broken up. The traitor has departed
on his walk of avarice and hate. The emblems of the cross and passion have been
exchanged and received. They descend
from that upper chamber, and as the
shadows of evening gather about them,
bend their steps to the Eastern ravine,
through which the Kedron pours its scanty
rill, and upward on the first ascending
slope of the Mount of Olives. There, a
little above the lowest part, was the Garden of Gethsemane, affording among its
olive shades a retirement suited for medita-
tion and prayer, to which Jesus had often
been accustomed to resort. But the ascent
hither is not silent. The voice of harmony
breaks upon the stillness of this memorable night. *They sang a hymn.* It is not
unlikely that they sang it as they walked.

Such use of religious song was not uncommon among the Hebrews, in going up to their solemn feasts; it has been adopted in later days, in the processional services of funerals and other solemn rites. At such an hour they doubtless sang from memory, and therefore something with which they were familiar. In sacred song, the least of all attendant charms is that of novelty. The words and tones which have received the additional loveliness of a thousand repeated associations, surpass all others in their power. Who knows, but that the hymn which they sang was one in which they had joined again and again with their Lord and Master? It is to be presumed that they all sang. Such was the custom of the Jewish Church. It is not hinted that Peter or James or John performed this service vicariously, as proxies for the rest. Which of the eleven, would willingly have been dumb, at such a moment, if only he comprehended the significancy of the hour? The voice which would have been out of tune, was absent, muttering, it may be, falsehood and perfidy in the ear of priests and pharisees. They sang a hymn. The disciples sang. Could we fully reproduce the strain, we should find in it probably nothing that meets the requisition of artistic taste. But it was assuredly elevated by the high solemnity of the scene, and broken into tremulous notes by the gush of pensive emotion.

JESUS SANG. This is a point not to be forgotten. Though not expressly said, it is distinctly implied. That sacred voice, which spake as never man spake, now poured forth the sentiments of an unblemished devotion, in the hour of all others the most pregnant and affecting. If feeling be the soul of song, there must have been conveyed into those notes a world of mysterious meaning. Is it wrong to wish that we could have listened to that voice? Yet we might have listened and been no better. How often had Judas heard the words of blessing from those lips—yet presently he is coming to profane them by his hellish kiss! Let us not push our inquiries into that which is not for edification, as being unrevealed. The fact that Jesus sang, is basis enough for certain reflections, which we desire shortly to build upon it.

More profitable is it to inquire what
was the subject of their song. 'They sang
a hymn.' Our modern acceptation of the
term is somewhat restricted. It was not
so in ancient times. Any religious compo-
sition adapted to singing was called a hymn.
Some have endeavoured to limit it to a
special class of Hebrew odes; but without
sufficient reason. The presumption is strong,
that they sang one of the inspired Psalms.
These were employed in the glorious worship of the temple. For this very purpose the heavenly inspiration came upon
Moses, David, Asaph, and other rapt seers
and poets. To this day the Psalter stands
as the great treasury of praise and prayer,
the authentic liturgy of the Church, which
can never grow obsolete; which presents
every varying mood of holy experience;
and by its divine flexibility and expansion
is equally suited to every revolving period
of the body of Christ. It almost seems as
if by a wise provision, the later psalms,
which are triumphal and jubilant, as if
for a palm-bearing multitude and an accompaniment of harp and cymbal, should
stand last in the collection; as too much

beyond our common experience to be in
unison with the frames of a striving and
militant church, and so awaiting a day
when the latter glory shall be fitly cele-
brated by anthems of loftiest joy and
exultation. But the psalms are not all
rapturous. The chords are sometimes
touched to the softest notes of penitence
and sorrow. And hence in their wonderful
modulations from confession to praise, they
suit themselves to all conditions of believers and the church. By the Israelitish
worshipper, they were sung without metre
and without rhyme; just as they stand in
our Hebrew Bibles. In this way were
they used by early Christian assemblies.
And there is no reason why our admirable prose version should not be so used
now, except our fond attachment to the
tradition of a metrical paraphrase. There
can be conceived no mode of singing God's
praise, more simple, grave, impressive and
truly Protestant, than the chanting of the
very words of Scripture by all the voices
of a congregation. Such—almost beyond a
doubt—was the sacramental hymn after
this first communion. The Psalms are full

of passages which relate to Messiah, and to this particular stage in his humiliation. It is most natural to think that some one of these was adopted by our blessed Master, at this moment of tenderness. There are numerous psalms, to which we can affix no clear, consistent meaning, until we regard the sacred poet as speaking in the name of Messiah; and it is remarkable how many such passages have reference to his death, and even to its lesser circumstances. Conjecture is not wrong, if we do not erect its results into divine certainties. May not the hymn have been the xxiid Psalm? beginning with words which thrill the soul: "My God, my God, why hast thou forsaken me!" What a touching anticipation of the cross, in v. 8th, "He trusted in the Lord that he would deliver him;—let him deliver him, seeing he delighted in him." Or the 18th, "They part my garments among them, and cast lots upon my vesture."—Or who shall say that it was not the lxixth psalm? From such lips, what a pathos in the lamenting notes: "The zeal of thine house hath eaten me up; and the reproaches of them tha⁺ reproached thee are fallen upon me. Reproach hath broken my heart, and I am full of heaviness; and I looked for some to take pity, but there was none;. and for comforters, but I found none; they gave me also gall for my meat; and in my thirst they gave me vinegar to drink." Or peradventure, by that Kedron, he may have sung in words of the cxth Psalm, "The Lord hath sworn, and will not repent, Thou art a priest forever, after the order of Melchisedek. He shall drink of the brook in the way; therefore shall he lift up the head." But whatever may have been the burden of that parting song, we know that they "sang a hymn" before they went into the Mount of Olives.

1. In these words there is a fearful import. They went out into the mount—they went to Gethsemane—they went to the scene of agony. The passion of our Lord, in both its principal parts, took place beyond the walls of the Holy City, as if to add new ignominy to the humiliation of his sin bearing. "For the bodies of those beasts, whose blood is brought into the sanctuary by the High Priest for sin, are

burned without the camp;" the typical
vicariousness of the suffering having tainted,
as it were, the sacrifice with imputed
guilt. "Wherefore," adds the Apostle to
the Hebrews, "Jesus also, that he might
sanctify the people with his own blood,
suffered without the gate." To suffer thus,
he was now going. There was a full fore-
sight of all that was to come upon him.
From the beginning his eye had steadily
contemplated it, and he had repeatedly
foretold it to his disciples. He had power
over his life, it was not taken from him
reluctantly or unawares. He advanced with
sublime composure to the altar, and was
not dragged thither as a shrinking or re-
sisting victim. "He is brought as a lamb
to the slaughter, and as a sheep before
her shearers is dumb, so he opened not
his mouth." This was therefore a moment
of deep sorrow. "Sorrow hath filled your
hearts:" he just now said to his disciples;
but what must have filled his own? The
skirt of that dense cloud, into which he
was entering, must have cast over him
some of its awful obscuration. For it was
but a few moments, before he was pros-

trate on the earth, his soul exceeding sorrowful, even unto death. For this he was now going to the Mount of Olives; to agony as yet unknown in the universe, and never to be repeated. And yet, thus going, *they sang a hymn.*

2. Is it not a fair conclusion, that sacred song adapts itself to seasons of the deepest grief? It is true the Apostle James says, "Is any afflicted, let him pray —is any merry let him sing psalms." But the voice of melody is not confined to the expression of joy, but by its admirable versatility is peculiarly fitted to convey sadness and despondency. Music and poetry agree in this. When the inspiration of soul is present, the attempt to pour out our sorrows in verse and subdued song, is not affectation, but nature. The history of all poetic compositions shows us this. None are more memorable than such as in hours of grief have been pressed out of hearts swelling over with emotion. So it is also in the inspired psalms. Even when the captives hanged their harps upon the willows, and replied, 'How shall we sing the Lord's song in a strange land;'

they nevertheless did sing, and the utterance of their experience in exile is left to us, in that beautiful elegy, 'By the rivers of Babylon, there we sat down.' They wept, when they remembered Zion, but as they wept, they sang. Religious sorrow occupies many of the Psalms of David; especially in their beginnings; for it is instructive to mark, how almost always the key changes, and how by a spiritual modulation, the song which begins in lamenting ends in praise; through the tender mercies of Him who giveth 'beauty for ashes, the oil of joy for mourning, and the garment of praise for the spirit of heaviness.' On this point great errors prevail, so that many Christians would no more think of psalmody than of feasting, in their hours of distress. And the mistake has perhaps been fostered by the manner of our ordinary singing in God's worship—so cold, hard, dry and mechanical, that it never suggests itself as the utterance of gentler and melting emotions. But could we use this means of grace according to its intention, and according to its marvellous capacity of varied expression, we should find

it the fittest and only perfect channel of
sentiments too sacred for the harsher in-
tonations of ordinary speech. Music has
its vehicles for the thoughts of the bur-
dened, the penitent, the heart broken and
the dying. Soft are the tones and wailing the key, when David murmurs, as the
chords of the harp scarcely add their re-
sonance—"My life is spent with grief, and
my years with sighing: my strength faileth
because of mine iniquity, and my bones
are consumed." "Forsake me not, O Lord,
O my God, be not far from me. Make
haste to help me, O Lord, my salvation."
"My heart is sore pained within me; and
the terrors of death are fallen upon me.
Fearfulness and trembling are come upon
me, and horror hath overwhelmed me.
And I said, Oh that I had wings like a
dove! for then would I fly away, and be
at rest!" The inspired devotions of the
Church, authorize the employment of song,
for the expression of our most subdued
emotions. If the Apostles sang, just as they
were going out into the mount of Olives;
if Jesus sang, at the moment just preceding his betrayal, agony and arrest; we

may surely feel justified, when deeply smitten and afflicted, if we resort to this medium of pouring forth sorrows which might otherwise prove inexpressible.

The lesson then seems to be unequivocally here: Songs of praise are not to be intermitted or silenced by seasons of great affliction. Here we have the disciples and their Lord on the verge of their great separation; yet they cause the voice of their praise to be heard. The further lesson is not to be mistaken; that when our religious feelings partake of sorrow and fear and compunction, we are not the less to utter them in spiritual song. It is often the way to the sweetest solace. And this is remarkably evinced by the experience of David. I take it for granted, that his compositions are so many leaves from this experience, and that he sang the psalms, which he afterward wrote down for us. I further suppose, that, under Divine inspiration, his mind passed through changes of mood and temper, varied and modified by the reflex operation of his own voice and instrument. Those who think this remark derogates aught from the directness of inspiration, can scarcely have considered the case of the ancient prophets; in which the illapses of Divine influence seem not only to have allowed, but demanded, the vehicle of music. So it was said by Samuel to Saul— "thou shalt meet a company of prophets coming down from the high-place with a psaltery and a tabret and a pipe and a harp before them; and they shall prophesy." 1 Sam. 10: 5 And when Elisha was about to receive the Divine influence and work a great miracle 2 Kings 3: 15 he called for music, saying "Now bring me a minstrel; and it came to pass, when the minstrel played, that the hand of the Lord came upon him." Thus too, while David was musing, the fire burned; and while he was singing, his soul passed through new frames, and often emerged from depths of horror into lofty thanksgivings.

He begins a psalm, 'Lord how are they increased that trouble me.' He ends it, 'Salvation belongeth unto the Lord: thy blessing is upon thy people.' He begins: 'O Lord rebuke me not in thine anger.' He ends: "The Lord hath heard the voice of my weeping." He begins: "How long wilt thou forget me, O Lord? for ever?" He ends: "I will sing unto the Lord, because he hath dealt bountifully with me." He begins: "Deliver me from mine enemies." He ends: "Unto thee, O my strength, will I sing; for God is my defence, and the God of my mercy." He begins: "Out of the depths have I cried unto thee, O Lord." And he ends: "Let Israel hope in the Lord, for with the Lord there is mercy, and with him is plenteous redemption." These were so many transitions of feeling, effected during holy song; and these songs are recorded for us, that in the use of them we may have a solace, and in like manner pass from grief to exultation. Be assured my brethren, there are uses of sacred music and uses of the psalms, in regard to inward experience, which many of us have yet to learn.

There is a principle involved in psalmody which extends widely in religion; it is that *our emotions are increased by due utterance.* All modes of utterance are not

equally suitable. For the expression of
sentiment and passion, it has been admitted, there is nothing comparable to the
musical voice. From neglecting this, there
are many whose hearts are like a spring of
which the flow is clogged by earth and
grass, so that it never has clear and unob-
structed flow. Not only is the actual
amount of their religious feeling unex-
pressed, but it abides at one point—it is
not increased—it has not the modifications
through which it would have passed by a
free and generous expression. Let it be
placed high among maxims for the im-
provement of piety, that our religious affections must have utterance. They must
not be pent up, lest they wither and de-
cline. It is so with those who restrain
prayer, or who indulge in no vocal prayer,
but restrict their devotions to silent mental acts. But much larger is the number
of those whose fountain dries up for lack
of a frank, large and hearty psalmody.
The great example before us, in this na-
scent condition of the Church, demonstrates
the importance of singing God's praise
together, even in hours of the greatest

tribulation. Which of us has not some shortcomings to confess, in regard to this duty? How apt are we to feel as if pain and sadness absolved us from the tribute of praise — at any rate, of social praise? When, in truth, we can never be brought into circumstances, in which our mercies do not immeasurably outnumber our trials; in other words, into circumstances where there is no call for thanksgiving. Early Christians judged otherwise. Not only were they speaking and admonishing one another, in psalms and hymns and spiritual songs; but when cast into dungeons and their feet in the stocks, "at midnight Paul and Silas prayed and sang praises unto God, and the prisoners heard them."

The particular mention of this hymn by two of the Evangelists, amidst the very record of our Lord's death, shows clearly that sacred praise harmonizes well with all the facts and all the doctrines of the atoning work. As has been said, many of the Old Testament psalms look forward prophetically towards these very events; and ever since the days of the Cross the dying sorrows of Jesus have formed a

chief portion of what have been sung by
Christian assemblies. It is truly delightful to observe, that even amidst all the
errors and superstitions of the Latin
Church, the death of the Redeemer has
still held its place in the hymns of the
people. The same, without need of quali-
fication, is true of the era of the Reformation. In her better days, Germany,
above all countries, was rich in evangelical hymns, and especially in those which
take us to Gethsemane and Golgotha. It
is only when the death of Christ becomes
a secondary matter, and his divinity is denied, that Socinian criticism begins to
amend the hymn-book, (as in some Euro-
pean churches) and weaken or remove all
expressions of love to a Divine and dying
Saviour. When the heart is full of faith
and worship, it will, sitting at the foot of
the Cross, long for the twofold wings of
poetry and song, to rise and soar to the
height of such praise as befits the wondrous work of redemption. In our own
favoured tongue, Watts and Wesley and
Toplady have aided us with strains, which
either in public or in private, aid our

thoughts and lift up our devotions. We
are familiar, from childhood, with their
words; but O for a coal from off God's
altar, to touch our lips and inflame our
hearts to praise!

And when they had sung an hymn
they went out into the Mount of Olives.
That is, they engaged in this act of worship, the only one of the kind recorded of
our Lord, at a time immediately between
the first Eucharist and the mysterious
agony of the Garden. What could be a
stronger argument for the authority and
fitness of *sacred song, in connexion with
sacramental communions!* The ordinance
was incomplete, until they had sung a
hymn. With the anguish, the strong crying and tears, and the bloody sweat full
in view, Christ will not go to them, before
he has mingled his voice with that of his
disciples, in audible praise. What a rebuke to those, who look on this part of
worship as secondary, as a mere appendage,
which they may observe or omit at pleasure, or as something which they are only
to witness, without any attempt at participation! For a service which is named the

Communion, nothing can be more appropriate than fellowship of praise. According to our mode of conducting Divine services, in other parts of worship all are silent but the officiating minister; but in psalmody all voices have the privilege of joining. And when the psalm is well chosen, and the heart attuned, what on earth can more nearly emulate the unity of heaven!

It is not unimportant to observe, that the little group who united in this sacramental hymn, were frail and imperfect men like ourselves. At this moment, no doubt, their hearts were deeply possessed with attachment to their Lord, and apprehensions more or less clear of what was soon to befall him. But their frames, like ours, were fitful and inconstant. After a little, while their Lord was in his agony, several of them were asleep. Somewhat later all forsook him and fled. And when a remnant was rallied, the foremost among them denied him repeatedly and with imprecation. This may serve us as an admonition, that sacramental fervours are not to be rested in, and that we need perpetual renewals of grace. But now, we would fain believe, there was as true a unison of sentiment as of psalmody. One voice there was, we know assuredly, which then broke the silence of the vale, in a flow of devotion which was absolutely perfect, in kind and in degree. The human soul of Jesus offered itself up, in a worship which was immaculate, sublime, and infinitely acceptable to God. This was true of all his prayers, for example, in solitude, upon mountains, long before day. When now, leading his sorrowing flock, he woke the echoes of crags and olive-groves, with the voice of praise, he left a pattern to his church, which we should warmly imitate. And O my brethren, how earnest should be our desires for more of the grace of real praise! The defect in this particular is alarming. There may be a pure creed, an able ministry, a decorous attendance, strict observance of the Sabbath, punctual resort to ordinances — and yet utter deadness in associate homage to our God and Saviour. How often is public prayer a mere performance, in which the officiating minister is left alone, to be listened to, if not disre-

garded. There are no sympathies of the
brethren, no breathings of common desire,
no silent, unutterable wrestlings of soul.
How often, in particular, is the psalmody
of God's house, a partial, scanty, unmeaning
utterance.

If forced to avow what is my growing
conviction, it would be this: we never shall
know the joys of the sanctuary, until there
be poured out upon us a new baptism in
regard to fellowship of adoration, love and
praise. We talk of our need of revival
in many things—and justly—but what we
greatly need is *a revival of the spirit of
worship.* How new a face would instantly
be put upon our solemn gatherings, if
whole assemblies, as the heart of one man,
were touched with an apprehension of a
present God, and not only individually but
jointly, were sending up the volume of
sanctified harmony, sometimes in tender
moanings like the dove, sometimes in pro-
foundest awe, sometimes in rapturous joy,
but all together and all accordant, not a
heart unmoved, and not a voice silent!—
Is it a vain fancy to think that such days
will come? Nay, brethren, unless we live

in perpetual delusion concerning the latter glory of the Church, there will be such a renewal of the spirit of worship, as in a thousand places the voice of joy shall be in the tabernacles of the righteous. Then shall God's praise—the highest employment of human tongues—ascend with such richness and volume, that a day in God's courts shall be better than a thousand. Then shall worshipping multitudes go up to the sanctuary of God their exceeding joy, with as much eagerness as now they press in throngs to amusements and festivities—but O with how great an increase of holy pleasure! Then shall the world without see and know that God is with us of a truth, and recognize that there is happiness in glorifying the name of God. The millennial church shall lift up heart and voice, in that new era, with a transcendent enthusiasm of pure bliss, far beyond all our present conceptions.—But however distant may be this day, and whether we live to see it or not, there is a world, where, if found faithful by grace, we shall hear and join the praises of the same Redeemer. For there the Church of the Old Testament and the New unite their voice, to sing "the song of Moses and the Lamb." Amidst much that is obscure in the Apocalypse, one thing is as clear as day, that in the heavenly state there shall be lofty, joyous, and perpetual praise of Christ. John heard them, "saying with a loud voice, Worthy is the Lamb that was slain, to receive power and riches and wisdom and strength and honour and glory and blessing." He saw also the great company, "having the harps of God," singing "Great and marvellous are thy ways, Lord God Almighty, just and true are thy ways, thou King of saints." O for some earthly prelibation of those joys! O for some sincere and hearty and unanimous anthems in the Church below!

V.

THE CRUCIFIXION.

THE CUCKOOS

THE CRUCIFIXION.

LUKE 23 : 33.

"And when they were come to the place which is called Calvary, there they crucified him."

WHEN Pilate had yielded to the tumultuous demands of the populace, and given up our blessed Lord Jesus to be scourged and mocked, the infuriated multitude led him away to be crucified. Taking from his lacerated body the royal purple which they had thrown over him in ridicule of his kingship, they clothed him in his own humble raiment and seamless coat. At the same time, and to add ignominy, they conducted two malefactors, destined to the same death. While this sad procession was leaving the eastern part of the city, we have reason to believe that Judas Iscariot was lying a ghastly corpse, having been driven to suicide by his despair. The street leading through the city and beyond the wall of that day has been well called the Way of Sorrows. It conducted them to a spot, never called a hill in the Scriptures, and still less a mount, named the place of Skulls, Golgotha, or in Latin Calvary. On the way to suffering it was the inhuman custom to lay the instrument of death as a burden on the prisoner. In this case there had been such an accumulation of enfeebling causes, in Gethsemane, the courts, and the place of bloody scourging, that our Lord sank under the weight. Even the transverse beam, supposing this to have been the burden, was too much for his sinking humanity. They therefore dragged into their service an African, of Cyrene, who was just then returning from the fields. The name of this man and his sons have thus found a place within the sacred record. We may conjecture that he was suspected of some sympathy or connexion; and it was his honour to follow Jesus, sustaining at least the end of the cross. The way was swoln with a pressing multitude, and among them were many women, friends of the Lord, unshaken by the sudden fanaticism, and pouring out cries of lamentation. Jesus heard these wailings and turned upon them his sorrowing and benignant eyes, saying, Daughters of Jerusalem, weep not for me; that is, your grief though kindly and pious is not founded on a full comprehension of this event; for I suffer that which I came into the world to endure, willingly offering this sacrifice. But weep for yourselves and for your children, that is, Your city and land must shortly suffer the vengeance of Almighty God for this and other crimes.

On arriving at the fatal spot, they hurried the preparations for a shameful and lingering death. And here we may pause a little to inquire what is meant by crucifixion. It is above all necessary that we discharge from our minds all those modern and sentimental decorations which men have hung about the cross; making it the symbol of salvation, borrowing its shape for majestic cathedrals, setting it up in gold and gems, and painting it on banners and armorial shields. These are associations posterior to the great oblation. Not such

was the rugged tree which was now to
be let down into its rocky socket; and
which was viewed by that glaring crowd,
as similar assemblages in our day regard
the scaffold, the halter and the gallows.

Crucifixion was preeminently an ignominious and most excruciating mode of
death; common among the Romans (till
the reign of Constantine,) and from them
transferred to Judea as a Roman province.
It appears from numerous Latin works that
it was inflicted chiefly on slaves, and such
gross offenders as highway-robbers and pi-
rates. Upon one thus suspended on a rack
by transfixed hands and feet, death came
on by frightful tortures. Ancient writers
tell us that it was commonly a suffering
for twelve hours, though in rare cases extended to more than twice that length of
time. The description of what learned
men give us as the series of mortal symp-
toms would harrow the feelings without
edification of heart.

Such was the punishment decreed to our
meek and innocent Redeemer. Among the
customs prevailing where this barbarous
penalty was known, it was usual to mingle

for the criminal a cup of strong wine with drugs. The officials gave our Lord vinegar mingled with gall, which he tasted but put away from him. The soothing potion of wine and myrrh, by whomsoever offered, he absolutely rejected. At the third hour, or nine o'clock of the day which we name Friday, Jesus was nailed to the cross, between the malefactors. No doubt this was studiously intended to exhibit him as the chief of sinners. And the Scripture was fulfilled which saith, "And he was numbered with the transgressors." Above his head was the title or inscription, in the three languages most known, Jesus of Nazareth, King of the Jews. Thus lifted up, in pangs which we cannot understand, and amidst inward sorrows communicable to no creature, our Lord opened his sacred lips with this utterance, "Father, forgive them, for they know not what they do!"

But about the very time when the forgiving Lamb of God was uttering this prayer for his murderers, the soldiers at the foot of the cross were dividing his garments as so much booty, and even gambling for that peculiar vestment which

being woven in one piece could not be
divided. This also had been predicted by
David, when he said in the name of the
Messiah Ps. 22 : 18 "They divided my
garments among them and cast lots upon
my vesture." The place of execution was
filled with such crowds as always gather
at scenes of blood, swelled in this instance by the paschal solemnity. The populace as they pressed forward and gazed,
and the multitudes who passed by in a
living stream, made a jest of these agonies, reviled our Lord, and nodded their
heads in derision, crying, Ah "thou that
destroyest the temple and buildest it in
three days, save thyself. If thou be the
Son of God, come down from the cross."
Men of higher rank, in church and state,
encouraged this scoffing, and said "He
saved others, himself he cannot save. If
he be Messiah, God's Elect One, King
of Israel, let him now come down from
the cross, and we will believe." But O
my brethren, if he had given this proof
of his power, which was easy, he had left
our salvation incomplete! The Gentile
guards united in the insults, and also ex-

claimed "If thou be the King of the Jews, save thyself!" One of the crucified malefactors, as if phrensied with anguish and depravity, took up the railing, and said, "If thou be the Messiah, save thyself and us." It seemed indeed as if the mission and work of Christ were utterly frustrated. But it was in this moment of desolation that our Redeemer asserted his sovereign power by absolving the repentant thief, and declaring "To-day shalt thou be with me in Paradise!"

The mind is somewhat relieved from the sight of malignant scoffers, by contemplating a little group around the cross, of those friends who had not been scattered by the panic of unbelief. It was Mary the mother of Jesus, another Mary her sister (the wife) of Cleopas, and a third Mary surnamed Magdalene. The beloved disciple, a man never terrified by dangers, a son of thunder, and one whose fiery zeal sometimes had needed the Master's rebuke, was likewise present. The eyes of Jesus bent towards this company, . which stood fascinated by grief and love, as he said,

" Woman, behold thy son !"—and to John,
" Behold thy Mother !"

Three hours of torture had now
elapsed, and it was noon; an interval
which measured by pain and the succession
of thought might be reckoned an age.
From this moment heaven gave signs of
awful sympathy with its incarnate Creator,
and there was darkness over all the land
for three hours, or till three o'clock of our
time. About the close of this supernatural
darkness, Jesus uttered a lamenting cry in
the words of the 22d Psalm, " My God,
my God, why hast thou forsaken me !"
Nothing could so express the depth of woe
into which our Lord plunged for our sake.
Say not that it conflicts with his divinity.
The difficulty here is only one of a number of difficulties, in an event which has
no parallel, and which baffles all human
speculation; since we cannot comprehend
even when we adoringly believe, how a
Divine Person could suffer penalty, or be
abandoned of God. Permanently abandoned he was not; sinfully abandoned he was
not; yet so far as the reception of heaven-

ly consolation is concerned, Christ was then and there forsaken. Separated from the godhead he was not; displeasing to God, he was not; but he was "made a curse for us," bore our imputed guilt, and as our substitute drank the cup of indignation. Let us not analyze what is infinitely beyond our reach, but bow the head and believe and love! The words Eli, Eli, being misapprehended by some present, led them to think it a cry for Elijah the prophet, who was predicted as his forerunner, who had appeared at the Transfiguration, and who the people thought was now summoned from paradise. But the atoning work was well nigh complete, and the Lord, knowing that all things were accomplished, gave vent to the burning demands of the human nature, and said, "I thirst." So also, in the Psalm twice quoted already, the ancient prophet says, "My tongue cleaveth to my jaws," and Ps. 69, "for my thirst they gave me vinegar to drink." One immediately ran to the vessel of vinegar which stood near, took a sponge, filled it with vinegar, and by means of a stalk of hyssop or a long reed, or both, reached it upward, to moisten the fevered lips of the dying Lamb of God: who when he had received it said, in a single emphatic word, "*It is finished!*" Then, crying with a loud voice, "Father into thy hands I commend my spirit!" he bowed his head, and expired. It was a voluntary breathing out of life; as he had said before "No man taketh my life from me, but I lay it down of myself." The term of agony as we observe was shorter than that of the malefactors beside him. This was the great climacteric of man's history. Since earth was formed, no event had been like this, that he who made it should die upon it. The moment was marked by portentous signs. The vail which secluded the Holy of Holies, a sacred tapestry never entered but by the High Priest, and by him once only in the year, was rent in sunder, from the top to the bottom. And this at the very hour of evening sacrifice, when the High Priest must have been standing at the golden altar. The old dispensation is no more. The old priesthood is superseded. The old sacrifices have lost their value, and are absorbed in the one great sacrifice for sin. There was an earthquake, and rocks were rent. As a consequence of this disturbance given to the sepulchral cemeteries, "many bodies of the saints which slept arose," and after the resurrection of Christ came out of their graves, entered the holy city, perhaps in undeniable glory as patriarchs and prophets may have been of the number, and as part of the rising Saviour's retinue appeared to many disciples.

But returning to our simple narrative. The Roman centurion, commanding the military guard, observing the words of Jesus in the article of death, looking on that countenance, in that instant of faith, consecration and divine love, and awed by the tokens in heaven and earth, 'glorified God,' saying "Certainly this was a righteous man"—nay—"Truly this man was the Son of God;" as he uniformly declared himself to be. And his soldiers assented, saying, "Truly this was the Son of God!" And all the people that came together at that sight, beholding the things which were done, smote their breasts and returned. And all his acquaintance, and many women, who, in Galilee had believed and followed and served him, including those before named, with Salome and the mother of James and John, the mother of James the Less and Joses, were witnesses of this event, from a suitable distance.

In long preparation of the Hebrew Church during many ages for this redeeming act, in which the Redeemer was to take on himself the penalty, the ignominy and curse, God here taught his peculiar nation to look on this mode of death as an abhorrence. Deut. 21, 22, 23. It was in the Law, ordained respecting one hanged on a tree, " His body shall not remain all night upon the tree—(for he that is hanged is accursed of God)—that thy land be not defiled." The Jews therefore, although they had brought the blood and wrath of the greater crime on their heads, were unwilling to incur the less. The next day was to be not merely their Sabbath, but a sabbath of peculiar sanctity, as succeeding their greatest feast, the Passover. The two malefactors were still lingering on their crosses, and seemed likely to survive the sunset, at which the Sabbath would begin. By Pilate's leave they therefore closed the sufferings of the robbers. But when the executioners, breaking the limbs of their victims, came to Jesus, they found it needless thus to rend his sacred body. His blessed spirit had already fled to paradise. And this was an intended coincidence with an Old Testament emblem. For concerning the lamb of passover, which age after age foreshadowed the Lamb of God, it was a solemn regulation Num. 11 : 12 "Not a bone of it shall be broken." Yet an inhuman soldier, with his spear, pierced that sacred side, and forthwith came there out blood and water. Great anatomists have written many learned treatises on this event, which may be profitably read; agreeing in this, that it was an infallible proof of death, and that our Lord could not have survived such a wound even if life had not been extinct. "And he that saw it (says the Apostle John, of himself) bare record, and his record is true, and he knoweth that he saith true, that ye might believe." It further accomplished those words spoken by Zechariah, concerning the conversion of Israel in the last days, "They shall look on him whom they have pierced."

I have accomplished my purpose, of giving a simple narrative of our Lord's death upon the Cross; being that particular event, which of all others he selected to be commemorated by a sacramental ordinance, by all disciples, through all ages; until He shall come again the second time without sin, unto salvation. (1.) You have before your minds, that event which is set forth in the Eucharist. The rite may have other bearings, but this is its primary intent, which cannot be neglected or overshadowed without doing a violence to the sacrament. Looking forward to this, a few hours before, on the evening of the paschal Thursday, he said as he gave the broken bread, "This do in remembrance of me; and as he gave the wine, This is my blood of the New Covenant shed for many, for the remission of sins." Put the two things together, and you perceive, that we approach this table aright, when we remember our Lord—when we remember him as shedding his blood for remission—that is when we remember him as an expiatory oblation. The broken bread, aids the remembrance; it is Christ's broken body. The fruit of the vine, the cup of blessing which we bless, aids the remembrance—it is the new testament in his blood. "This do ye, as often as ye drink it, in remembrance of me." Mere bread and wine, however consecrated, do not make a sacrament. There must be an eye of faith to look through and beyond the emblem and see Jesus Christ, visibly set forth, crucified among us. It is possible even to eat of this bread and drink of this cup 'unworthily.' The Corinthians were guilty of this very sin, "not discerning the Lord's body," not penetrating to somewhat beyond the common nutriment and refreshment of a repast, not seeing that all the virtue lay in the atoning death of the Son of God, exhibited and sealed to faith in this ordinance. All which brings us again to the important truth, that in partaking, we must bend all the perceptions of the soul on a single point, Christ on the Cross—Christ broken by the mighty arm of divine justice for

our sins—Christ pouring forth his blood as
the basis of that new covenant which gives
to many remission of sins. To this centre
or focal point of all theology, I invite your
regards this day. The voice of Jesus from
the accursed tree, calls to you in bewail-
ing but gracious accents, "Look unto me
and be ye saved, all ye ends of the earth."
Look then. Come hither with me, beloved
disciples—for the world without cares for
none of these things — come hither, and
draw more closely around the Cross. Say
with Moses, "I will now turn aside and
see this great sight." Lift up your eyes,
and fix them on the only begotten of the
Father full of grace and truth. Read in
those benign eyes, swimming in death, a
profound, a divinity of love, compassion and
saving grace, which death could not quench.
Catch those utterances of pity and forgiveness, which mingled with his personal la-
mentations. "Father forgive them"—"This
day shalt thou be with me"—"It is finished"—"Into thy hands I commend my
spirit."—Hearest thou? hearest thou? O
sinful soul? Hearest thou the *Gospel* of
salvation from the lips of dying love and

omnipotence? Can such expiation be unavailing—such prayers unanswered—such welcomes insincere? Need you any further demonstration of Christ's present readiness? "Greater love hath no man than this, that a man lay down his life for his friends." Can you doubt God's love? "God commendeth his love toward us, in that while we were yet sinners, Christ died for us." Dare you hesitate as to who are intended by this saving work? *You* are intended; unless you are one who has never sinned; and the message of the cross is a message to you, and offered to universal acceptance, to your present acceptance. "For this is a faithful saying, Christ Jesus came into the world to save sinners." Look steadily at this cross, and you will own its attractive virtue according to that word, "And I, if I be lifted up will draw all men unto me." Remember, remember Christ dying for your sins.

2. The view which we are to take of a dying Christ is not natural sympathy with his human sufferings. These were indeed great, unparalleled and unutterable. But it is observable that the bodily pangs

of our Lord are not made prominent in
the Scripture narrative; and this may account for the simplicity of the recital already given in the former part of this
discourse.   There are individuals, if we
should not rather say churches, in which
this merely natural apprehension of Jesus Christ and him crucified has been almost the whole of religion.   Imagination
has been called in to melt the affections,
and poetry, eloquence, painting and sculpture have lent their aid.   But piety of
this sort may attain any height and yet
be no quality of holiness.   There is little
devotion in a naked and passive sensibility.
A sacrament, or a sermon, like a mighty
work of art, may dissolve a hearer in tears,
and yet leave him no better.   Otherwise,
the most susceptible temperament would be
the criterion of the greatest saint; when
we know on the contrary that persevering
hatred of sin and devotion to God's service
exist in many who are little given to gusts
of natural passion.   Our Lord plainly dis-
suades us from this simply human and compassionate view of his death, by the words
which he turned and spake to the weeping

daughters of Jerusalem. Those pictures and graphic crucifixes therefore, not to speak of waxen mockeries and tragical stage representations, which have been common in Romish churches during their Passion week, are observed to leave the very crowds that weep and smite the breast ready next day to go about deeds of violence or license. And the same principle would apply to verbal painting, artful rhetoric, and such eloquence as should bring before the mind's eye the dying Saviour as if bleeding in our very presence. Heated imagination, in cases of enthusiasm and rapture, has still more vividly called up the apparition of Christ upon the cross; and this has been taken by some as the crowning evidence of their conversion. All in vain; if the matter goes no further. For can any art of pencil, of music, or of style attain to the reality there before the eyes of those who stood around our Saviour's Cross? And yet, some of these very persons "crucified the Lord of glory!" In the very presence of that divine countenance, and listening to the very tones of that heavenly voice, they drove the nails and urged the spear to the seat of life. Nor are we hastily to conclude that all who burst into tears at beholding the innocent bloodshedding of the Lord, were renewed in the spirit of their minds. Such emotions are certainly not wrong; it is admitted that they are natural. But we are in need of something that is beyond nature. Tender sympathies and gushing pity may even aid our religious affections; but they must not be rested in. And it is utterly vain and deceptive to make our thoughts terminate in the sufferings of Christ, however deeply we may sink under them, unless we pass through them all, to the mysterious intent and efficacy of his agony.

3. The death of Christ, exhibited in the sacrament, is to be viewed by FAITH. Here we pass from the region of nature to the region of grace. The faculty which looks through the elements of bread and wine, and through all outward pains of a holy being, is faith. It is faith, that beholds this spotless Lamb, laid on the altar of divine Justice. It is faith, that sees the penalty here exacted of the blessed Substitute. It is faith, that hears the invitation extended

to every sinner in the gospel. It is faith,
that perceives the salvation as complete,
suitable, available, present, made over, and
held out for the acceptance of the individual soul. It is faith, that actually accepts
it, laying the hand of appropriation on the
head of the unblemished victim that pal-
pitates beneath the sacrificial sword. And
it is faith, that renews these very acts of
reception, surrender, and adhesion, with
equal or increasing readiness, again and
again, through all the Christian life.—In
other words Faith 'discerns the Lord's
body;' faith receives it; faith feeds upon
it. The lively emblems of this holy table
are helps to faith. We believe the more
promptly and strongly, when we look on a
rite, instituted by the very hands which
were presently to be pierced for our sake,
and transmitted from that upper chamber
to this day, through every vicissitude of
persecution, division and error. And we
believe the more tenderly, and cling to our
faith the more earnestly, when we discover
in these symbols, not a sign merely, but a
seal, of divine appointment, pledging unto
us, and to each of us, who so eats and so

drinks, all the loving kindness and covenant grace purchased by the death of Christ.

4. Lastly; The true disciple is disposed to part with his sins at the Cross. That is to say, he exercises not only faith but repentance. There is no true repentance which does not spring from faith. Some people think they will repent first, and then come to Christ. Vain thought! As if one should forsake darkness first, and then come to the light. Conviction there may be, prior to believing, or remorse, compunction, fear, legal sorrow, but true repentance is "a tear that glistens in the eye of faith." And, as we learned long ago, Repentance unto life includes not only a true sense of sin, but an "apprehension of the mercy of God in Christ." For which cause many go all their life long without any tenderness of repentance, because they will not come to Christ; who is exalted a prince and Saviour "to give repentance and remission of sins." — The head becomes often as waters, and the eyes a fountain of tears, at the foot of the Cross; or (what most nearly resembles it) at the table of this sacrament. If you

behold Jesus "bruised for your iniquities" you have a reason for hating and forsaking sin, more powerful than the lightnings of Sinai. "Know ye not that so many of us as were baptized into Jesus Christ were baptized into his *death?*"* The system which we professed at our initiation was founded in that event. "Our old man is crucified with him, that the body of sin might be destroyed, that henceforth we should not serve sin." There is a sense in which we were put to death with Christ on the cross. The nails which fastened him there passed through us also. "For if one died for all, then all died." 2 Cor. 5 : 14.† Therefore Paul exclaims, "Henceforth let no man trouble me"—let none hinder me in the race of holy service— "for I bear in my body the marks, *stigmata*, of the Lord Jesus." "I am crucified with Christ—nevertheless I live; yet not I, but Christ liveth in me; and the life which I now live in the flesh I live by the faith of the Son of God, who loved me and gave himself for me."‡ Mark how

---

* Rom. 6 : 3.　　† See original.　　‡ Gal. 2 : 20.

he comes back to Christ's giving himself
up to death. The cause of Christ's death
and of all his sufferings was our sins. This
is brought palpably before us in the Lord's
Supper. We may therefore very properly
partake of this our New Testament passover, with "bitter herbs;" mourning over
our sins, as the true murderers of our
blessed Lord. And the sense of pardon
derived from believing apprehensions of his
dying love will be so far from hindering
this divorce between us and our sins, that
it will drive us with new impulsion to
effect it. The grace is infinite; but it is
the grace not only of justification but of
sanctification. "Shall we continue in sin
that grace may abound? God forbid!
How shall we who are dead to sin, live
any longer therein?" "Likewise reckon ye
also yourselves to be dead indeed unto
sin, but alive unto God through Jesus
Christ our Lord." The very profession of
faith, which we make at the Lord's Table,
implies our turning the back forever upon
the world, the flesh, and the devil. To
look with eyes of love on the Lord Jesus,
symbolically broken in this loaf and bleed-

ing in this cup—to gaze into the recesses and deep meanings of those eyes of divine pity and eternal love—is at one and the same time to swear allegiance, and yield yourself in espousals never to be broken. You cannot help it! If you hesitate, if you draw back, if you linger, if there is aught you love better—how is it possible that you can believe! Oh no! Faith will take no denial. She is a queenly Grace. She will bring you to Jesus. She will knit your hand to his. She will join you in a covenant never to be forgotten. By every pang that pierced his heart upon the cross, she will argue with you and constrain you to come out of the land of his enemies, and live forever under his rule. We take our stand as a family of brothers this day on this profession. By this Cross we are crucified unto the world, and the world is crucified unto us. This ordinance erects the Cross in the midst of our assembly. On this one point all eyes are fastened. Not only so, on this tree of death all of us are in a certain sense suspended. We are no more of the world, but of the cross. God forbid that we should glory save in the

Cross of our Lord Jesus Christ! This is to be made conformable to his death and to have fellowship with his sufferings. The vast atoning wonder, which eclipsed the day and cleft 'mountains and evoked the bodies of ancient saints from their sepulchres,' has meanings and virtues which Eternity holds in reserve. As the cherubim of glory stooped over the golden coronet of the Ark, so these "things Angels desire to look into."

"Angels that hymn the Great I Am
Fall down and veil before the Lamb."

Think you that heaven forgets the redemption of Golgotha! Hark! What voice is that which the beloved disciple hears, as he falls like one dead? "I am he that liveth and was dead; and behold I live for evermore, Amen!" What vision is this which catches his eye in the midst of the throne and the cherubic beings? It is "a Lamb as it had been slain." What anthem echoes from the elders, when they come with harps and odors? "Thou wast slain, and hast redeemed us to God by thy blood, out of every kingdom and tongue and people and nation, and hast made us to our God, kings and priests, and we shall reign on the earth." And what ocean of harmonious song is this which surges in waves of adoration from the surrounding multitudinous circles, of ten thousand times ten thousand and thousands of thousands? "Worthy is the Lamb that was slain to receive Power, and Riches, and Wisdom, and Strength, and Honour, and Glory and Blessing!" Amen and Amen.

VI.

WATER AND BLOOD.

WATER AND BLOOD.

JOHN 19 : 34.

"But one of the soldiers with a spear pierced his side, and forthwith came there out blood and water."

In our meditations at the Communion we generally contemplate our blessed Lord as dying: here we look upon him as already dead. His bloodless lips were parted with the cry, "It is finished," and then he expired. No more imputed guilt, no more suffering; the payment has been made, the sacrifice has been laid on the altar. The cup which his Father gave him has been drunk to the dregs. Pale and cold, the lovely form hangs in the unmistakable attitudes of death. And this is recognized by the party of soldiers sent at the Jews' request, to save their high festival from the pollution which would have resulted

from the suspension of criminal corpses
over night. The malefactors had borne the
torture; and history shows us that victims
of the cross sometimes lingered for days.
It was necessary to put a cruel end to
their torment by a process having its tech-
nical name in Latin; not unlike the *coup
de grace*, or finishing stroke, of culprits
broken on the wheel. 'The tender mercies
of the wicked are cruel.' Yet, this very
violence fulfilled the word of Jesus to one
of the robbers, 'This day shalt thou be
with me in Paradise.' But the pure spirit
of the Divine Oblation in the midst has not
awaited such an outrage. Of the paschal
lamb, the type of this our Lamb of God,
it had been ordained, "A bone of him
shall not be broken." Also the Psalmist's
words have come true: "Thou keepest all
my bones, not one of them is broken."
Wounded, rent, sheeted in crimson, that
precious body nevertheless shall endure
neither fracture nor corruption. Yet the
awful, mystic murmurs of prophecy echo to
us from the recesses of the Old Testament,
with inklings of insult and wounding to
the heart of God incarnate. For God it

was who said: "And they shall look upon me whom they have pierced and they shall mourn." Hence our surprise may be lessened, when amidst the closing tortures of the thieves, a Roman soldier (the Longinus of legend) makes trial of Christ's death; as to its reality. Real indeed it was. Had he not said "I lay down my life—no man taketh it from me, but I lay it down of myself." "One of the soldiers with a spear pierced his side, and forthwith came there out blood and water." It is not said which side; the great masters of Romish art have chosen the right, in order perhaps to exhibit the event as purely miraculous; but learned conjecture has as generally settled upon the left. The fair, innocent, adorable body, thus lacerated, was now not sensible, but dead. If it had not been, this mortal thrust had completed the murder. Our witness is one who the day before had leaned upon that bosom, then warm with love and heaving with pity; one who, now fixed at the foot of the cross, supporting Mary the mother of Jesus, had just heard those lips say 'Behold thy mother.' v. 27. He marks a single circumstance, as unusual, memorable and significant; he marks it with a triple asseveration, v. 35, 36: "forthwith came there out blood and water." He marks it, as spiritually important, many years afterwards, when in old age, surviving all his brother Apostles, surviving Jerusalem itself, he writes: 1 Jo. 5: 6. "This is he who came by water and blood, even Jesus Christ, not by water only, but by water and blood." Such redoubling of statement, such solemnity of attestation, such mystery of application, may fully justify us in giving the point our most serious study.

Various have been the conjectures of science as to the source of this effusion. Infidels have denied that blood ever flows from the corpses of those who die from severe wounds. Even if this were so, as it is not, we should only be left to believe a miracle. Some have spoken of water in the pericardium or membranous sac which contains the heart. The subject has been treated by medical authors of the highest rank. The soundest conclusion seems to be this: In cases of violent death from torturing extension of the muscles, the blood may continue fluid, even after dissolution, and may readily escape passively from the great vessels. The stroke of the Roman lance was not any slight puncture or superficial wound; if it had been such, Jesus would never have said to unbelieving Thomas, 'Reach hither thy hand and *thrust it into my side*." The spear-head made open laceration and wide entrance; producing a twofold effect; first reaching nearer parts where the serous or watery portion of the blood found escape, and then plunging more deeply in the region of the heart, and making way on its return for the proper crimson tide. "Forthwith came there out blood and water." It is especially to be remarked, that Scripture says nothing as to the quantity of either; whether great or small. The fact arrested the upturned gaze of the group below, and imprinted its image for life upon the loving Disciple, who, employing terms of modesty concerning himself, says: "And he that saw it bare record, and his record is true, and he knoweth that he saith true, that ye might believe."

There is a philosophy my brethren, which has tampered with the interpretation of the

Word; which has climbed to chairs of
theology; which has installed chill rationalism in the pulpit; a philosophy which
would drain off the last juices from the
clusters of inspiration, and rob every bleeding type in Leviticus of its Christ-ward
pointing. It is the philosophy of Socinian
coldness and baptized infidelity. Seeing no
substitution, imputation, penal suffering, or
expiatory sacrifice in the Cross, it naturally
beholds no more than a singular patholo-
gical phenomenon at this opened side.
God grant us eyes to look more deeply,
even into that mystery which the Apostle
deemed worthy of his rehearsal, when he
wrote: "there are three who bear witness in earth, the Spirit, and the water,
and the blood: and these three agree in
one." The warm African imagination of
St. Augustin* carries him into a flight in
which we may not all follow him, but
which yet suggests the hidden meaning of
the signal event. This eloquent father,
preaching nearly fifteen hundred years ago,
thus spoke: "It is finished, said He, and

* Serm. V.

bowed his head and gave up the ghost;
as though he had endured till all was finished. When he so willed, he gave up his
soul. *He* therefore was *God:* they who
were crucified beside him were men. He
dies at once, they more slowly. And when
it was ordered that the bodies should be
removed on account of the sabbath, the
officers found the thieves living, and brake
their legs, but the Lord already departed.
Yet one of them with a lance pierced his
side, and forthwith came there out blood
and water. Lo the price paid for thee!
For what is flowing from this side, but the
mystery (sacramentum) which believers receive? Spirit, Water, Blood. Spirit, which
the [dying Jesus] breathed out: Blood
and Water flowing from his side. Signifying that of this very blood and water the
church is born. And *when* was it that
blood and water issued thus? It was when
Christ [our second Adam] was sleeping
upon the cross; just as, of old, Adam in
Paradise was laid in deep slumber, and
from his side *Eve* was taken. Lo the
price paid for thee!" Earlier than Augustin, another African Christian, like all

the ancients loving to dwell on the "Cross and Passion," thus speaks in his characteristic and almost extreme way: "Christ says Tertullian* had come, by water and blood, that he might be baptized with water and glorified with blood; and in order to render us by water his called, and by blood his chosen, he sent forth these two baptisms from the wound of his pierced side, so that those who should believe in this blood might be washed with this water, and likewise that they who should be cleansed with this water might drink of this blood." You catch the allusion at once — it is frequent in that Christian antiquity which our age neglects; it is like the famous saying, that out of the side of Jesus issued the two Sacraments; Baptism, the sacrament of water, the Lord's Supper, the sacrament of blood. More rigorously stated, perhaps we should err less in saying, Out of that blessed, violated side issued twin emblems, parallel with the New Testament Sacraments; and symbolizing the same glorious

* De Bap. c. 16.

benefits. My brethren we have this day the privilege of approaching both. Let us, in reliance on Divine aid, contemplate the twofold lesson. It will prepare the way for our better understanding of the matter, connected thus with the very heart of religion, if we return for a moment to the threefold witness. 1 Jo. 5 : 7.". As this witnessing may be viewed from two different sides; either as outwardly proposed for the conviction of men, or inwardly applied for the consolation of believers, so we think those three Witnesses may be regarded under a like twofold aspect, that is as testifying within or without. Thus by the Spirit (that witnesseth) we understand the power and efficacy of the Holy Ghost, as well outwardly working by the Word, as inwardly effectual in the heart. By the Water, first the sacrament of Baptism, administered in the Church under the symbol of water and then (that which Baptism signifies) its verity, which is wrought in the heart by the grace of regeneration. By the Blood, first the sacrament of the Eucharist, 1 Cor. 10 : 16 which is the communion of the blood of Christ, and then

the grace of justification, or remission of
sins in the blood of Christ, which is sealed
in this sacrament.   And thus, we may in
a sense note six several parts of this testimony, not differing totally in kind, but
mutually answering and subordinate to each
other.   For the external are symbols of
internal things; and the internal are the
verity and reality signified by the external
things."*

But let us briefly consider apart the
two truths set forth in the drops which
issued from the side of Jesus. "Forthwith
came there out blood and water;" or penetrating to the hidden sense: THE TWO
GREAT BENEFITS WHICH WE OWE TO OUR
DYING LORD ARE EXPIATION AND SANCTIFI-
CATION, Expiation by blood, Sanctification
by water.   You will observe a difference
in the two writings of John, as to the
order of statement.   In the Epistle it is,
"this is He that came by *water and blood*."
Our text gives the order of appearance in
the actual fact, which is at the same time
the order of application in the sinner's

* 4 Turretin, 115.

consciousness; seeing he first comes to the blood of Jesus for pardon and then to the sense of being purified. But in the other statement the regenerating influence is placed first, which is also the order of the two sacraments, and in a sense the order of nature, because the soul is changed before it believes unto justification. We will follow the words before us.

I. EXPIATION. Blood has this meaning in all the Old Testament, the language of which was, "Without shedding of blood is no remission." All the levitical rites, during centuries, were preparing the Church to comprehend this bloodshedding upon the Cross. Every lamb which throbbed, bled and died under the priestly knife; every baptism with the hyssop dipped in "the bowls of the altar," every affusion of the sinner, the congregation or the mercy-seat, drew expectant eyes towards the Lamb of God who taketh away the sin of the world. Nor is that system of types obsolete, as a means of instruction. For although the Old Testament is dark until we read the New, yet the latter gives a clew with which to thread all the labyrinth of Mosaic rites.

The first grand need which a returning sinner feels, is need of reconciliation. Till relieved here, he can attend to nothing else, not even the blessed work of the sanctifying Spirit. He has sinned against the glorious God. Wrath looks down upon his hell-deserving heart. Guilt stains and defiles his conscience. The cry within his bosom is, "Take away the vengeance of God—give me reconciliation — standing in his presence — justifying righteousness or you offer me all the rest in vain!"

This demand of the heart only echoes the higher demand of infinite Justice. All ages were in travail with this unuttered secret. Rivers of blood flowed through the temple courts of Moriah, to prepare for Gethsemane and Golgotha. Here, amidst earthquake and darkness, the marvellous achievement takes place. "Messiah is the end of the law for righteousness." The mystery is revealed. The Holy of holies is made accessible. Its golden glories are now as a common thing, in comparison with the divine reality. And so the vail of the temple is rent in twain from the top to the bottom. The hour has come. The Son of Man is glorified. That immaculate Spirit passes away from pain forever. The emblematic blood is forced from his sacred side. Let me repeat the saying of Augustine: 'Behold, O sinner, the price of thy redemption!' O if the true protomartyr John the Baptist looked down upon the Cross from the paradise to which he had been borne out of his own blood ... must he not with rapture and awe have repeated his Gospel, Behold the Lamb of God? Now is he lying dead on the divine altar. The work is complete in the court without. The High Priest has gone in with the sacrificial blood to sprinkle it upon the mercyseat, in the heavenly places not made with hands. But see! another John, stands all absorbed in wonder, grief, and believing love. He begins to comprehend the meaning of a thousand sayings of prophets and of his Lord. He catches an inspiration which, during a long pilgrimage, is to make him preeminently the apostle of love. He beholds the frame which he loved,

and with every fibre of which he is in
tender sympathy, convulsed into agonizing
distortion, stiffened by extension, marred
with gore, and stark in the chillness of
an evening from which the sun had so
long withdrawn himself. But even the
warmth of human love is swallowed up in
a holier sympathy. ' *My sins*, are visited
there!' "He is the Propitiation for our
sins; and not for ours only, but also for
the sins of the whole world."

In the solemn pathetic discourses of
primitive Christians, when they met to
commemorate the broken body and flowing
blood of Jesus, they doubtless pointed
to the holy sacrament as depicting the
event which we are considering. 'This
broken loaf,' they would say, 'recalls to
us the beloved side whose death-whiteness
was crimsoned with its heart's blood.' 'This
we do in remembrance of Him, in remembrance of a death fresh and recent; a
death to which we owe our soul's rescue
from wrath and curse. He bare our sins
in his own body on the tree. By these
stripes are we healed. It is Justification,
and of course the Pardon (that Justifica-

tion includes) which comes to us from the side of our Redeemer. Jesus is made sin for us, that we might be made the righteousness of God in him. It is the fundamental doctrine of our faith as sinners. Not only do we believe in God the Father, but in Jesus Christ his Son, who was conceived by the Holy Ghost, suffered under Pontius Pilate, was dead and buried." But there is another great benefit which we receive from Christ on the Cross:

II. SANCTIFICATION.—This is the natural significancy of Water in all the ceremonial hieroglyphic of the ancient rites. There were divers "washings" (*baptisms*), as the Apostle Paul writes. No figure could be more expressive, than cleansing of the body to represent the cleansing of the soul. And therefore we find the sacred writers sliding, as if unconsciously, from one to the other, and speaking of outward when they really mean inward washing. A Hebrew convert would especially do thus. Accustomed to the ceremonial ablutions, which relieved his conscience in regard to breaches of ritual holiness, he would recur to them, when he wished to feel and express the inward purity which they typified. Drawn to look into the true but invisible *Sanctum sanctorum*, he would follow with his eye the divine propitiatory Messiah, entering within the veil with the tokens of his bloody sacrifice; and so would fall in, as thousands must have done, with those glorious words, Heb. 10:19-22, "Having therefore, brethren, boldness to enter into the holiest of holies by the blood of Jesus, by a new and living way which he hath consecrated for us, through the vail, that is to say, his flesh; and having a HIGH PRIEST over the house of God; let us draw near with a true heart in full assurance of faith, having our hearts sprinkled from an evil conscience, and our bodies washed with pure water." I pray you Christian hearers lose not the phrase; but mark how New Testament experience uses Old Testament idiom; *our bodies washed with pure water.* "The like figure whereunto" we may without perversion of Peter's words add, "doth now save us, even Baptism; not the putting away of the filth of the flesh, but the answer of a good con-

science toward God; by the resurrection of
Jesus Christ." 1 Peter 3 : 21. Nothing
but the most extreme bias of a foregone
conclusion and partisan zeal for a darling
form, could ever have led any to maintain
that the idea of cleansing is not essential
to baptism. Washing, not dipping, is the
primary notion. Ancient bathing was seldom by immersion, even when great lavers
were used. The classical scholar knows
that the *Baptisterion* of the Greeks was a
small vessel. Scripture lays no stress on
the mode of signifying a cleansing application of water, still less makes it essential.
Cleansing operations are variously set forth
in emblem. Of the great Laver of brass,
it is written, "Aaron and his sons shall
wash their hands and their feet thereat."
Ex. 30 : 19. Of an unclean person, Lev.
15 : 30 " he shall wash his clothes and bathe
his flesh in running water." Of ceremonial
defilement by corpses Num. 19 : 18 "And a
clean person shall take hyssop and dip it
in the water, and sprinkle it upon the
tent." The minds of the people were im-
bued with these symbols of purification, so
that bedewing with water signified to them

the sanctifying influences of the Holy
Spirit. Thus were they prepared to rejoice in the prophetic promise Ezek. 36 : 25
"Then will I sprinkle clean water upon
you and ye shall be clean." The asper-
sion or affusion of water in the Old Testament signified the making clean; so did
the holy drops which followed the cruel
spear; so does the sacramental water which
falls upon the brow.

Our salvation, Christian brethren, had
been incomplete, if Jesus had stopped short
with pardon. By atonement he procures
another infinite good. In justification, we
receive a change of standing, in reference
to justice and law; but we need a change
of nature and life. Our blessed Lord did
not die to keep us in an eternity of sinning. Nor yet did he secure for us remission of God's wrath, simply that we
might henceforward advance on our own
account, and have a new trial. Nay; we
should not have stood firm an hour. He
came and suffered, moreover, for a higher
end, than to afford us the greatest motive
to be holy. These are not God's ways.
This Redeemer who hangs dead upon the

tree has endured this death out of infinite
love to holiness and infinite regard for the
glory of the Father. "This is he that
came by water," (more exactly "with water.") This is he that came with sanctifying influence; that "he might purify to
himself a peculiar people, zealous of good
works." While we look upon the baptis-
mal flow which spreads over his side, we
recognize in it not merely the wounding
of a body which never knew sin, holy,
harmless and undefiled—but the pledge of
holiness in his people, as ensured by this
his sacrificial death. For by his Cross,
Jesus has made holiness desirable, possible
and certain. First, the Cross makes holiness desirable. There can be no stronger
motive to inward purity than that which
is presented in the death of Christ. "The
love of Christ constrains us, because we
thus judge, that if one died for all, then
all died, and that he died for all that they
which live should no longer live unto themselves, but unto him that died for them
and rose again." If you would be moved
to holy living, self-denial and mortification
of the flesh — gaze upon the Cross. Con-

sider that it was sin which crowned that head, fixed those hands and feet with spikes to the tree, and rent its sacrilegious way into the chambers of that holy side. If indeed it should be your purpose to harbor sin, you will not be able to bear the sight; you will turn away to other thoughts; you will avoid those chapters of the Gospel which treat of the Passion, you will absent yourself from the communion of his body and blood. For the more a believer contemplates the Cross, the more will he long to be holy, and to purify himself even as He is pure.

Secondly, The Cross makes holiness possible. Even if we were cleansed from the guilt of sin, that is, freed from being liable to punishment, the heart and conscience would cry out for more. There must be water as well as blood, purity as well as pardon, power to obey as well as sense of escape. This power is only from the Holy Spirit of God, procured in the way of purchase, by Christ's obedience unto death; and claimed by him on his ascension into heaven. Jesus, as Mediator, has merited that the Spirit of holiness should be given to his people. Before he suffered, he instructed them, that unless he suffered, this Comforter would not come. At Pentecost there was a signal epiphany of the Spirit; but not confined to that day. "He that believeth in me" said the Lord, "from within him shall flow rivers of living water." "This spake He of the Spirit which they that believe on him should receive: for the Holy Ghost was not yet given, because that Jesus was not yet glorified." But now that he has been glorified (in the affecting sense which he has himself explained to us, Jno. 13:31) the Holy Ghost is given to all believers, to enable them to live unto God. This power therefore we receive by the death of Jesus. Thirdly, the Cross makes holiness certain. Not merely desirable by giving motive; not merely possible, by giving aid; but infallibly certain, by giving pledge and assurance. The salvation which Christ has bought by his most innocent and infinitely precious dying, is not a loose contingency, a chance of doing better, a probability suspended on the believer's mutable will; but a true and finished redemption, securing the grace

which shall sweetly but assuredly fix that
will. Look at the heavenly chain, remark
how its golden links hang together, and
consider which of them you would strike
out. Rom. 8 : 30 "Moreover whom he
did predestinate, them he also called: and
whom he called, them he also justified;
and whom he justified, them he also glorified." The pledge issued from that blessed
side. "If one died for all, then all died."
By the effect of the covenant, "we are crucified with Christ;" we die unto sin; ceas-
ing more and more from the practice of
it. The Spirit of holiness causes us to love
and practise what is pleasing to God. As
surely as any man believes in the Lord
Jesus Christ, so surely shall he be saved;
and saved from sin. Thus the cross makes
our sanctification certain. But we must
hasten towards our conclusion. We have
beheld issuing from our Saviour's pierced
side both blood and water. We have
learnt in the school of types that these
denote our Justification and our Sanctification; and that the Christian sacraments, of
the Eucharist and Baptism denote the
same. Take the two together, and they

comprehend our salvation. If Christ "is made unto us," first, "righteousness" and then "sanctification," we have all; at least in its beginning, in pledge, in hope, and in certitude. Heaven itself is only the perfection of peace with God, and the consummation of holiness. Neither in heaven nor earth can we have one, without having something of the other. To seek for pardon, without hatred of sin or a desire to be delivered from it, is the delusion of antinomian hypocrisy. "In this the children of God are manifest, and the children of the devil; whosoever doeth not righteousness is not of God, neither he that loveth not his brother." 1 Jno. 3: 10 If God has touched us by his Spirit, if he has made us know the plague of our own heart; if he has so laid the plummet of the Law beside the crookedness of our life, as to cause despair of creature-help; if he has so revealed himself in the majesty of his holiness, that we have abhorred ourselves and repented in dust and ashes;— then, at the Cross, we have craved both blood to expiate and water to cleanse. So did the Hebrew penitent at God's altar;

he craved the drops which had just gushed from the lamb of sacrifice; he craved the baptism which should afford cleansing to his ceremonial vileness. The penitent king, stained with adultery and murder, groans forth a twofold wish: "Purge me with hyssop and I shall be clean; wash me, and I shall be whiter than snow." True faith looks toward the crucified Redeemer for both. God is offended, and of our own stores we can make no reparation or atonement: but "the blood of Jesus Christ his Son cleanseth us from all sin." It is because we have approached the Saviour, that we desire to approach the sacrament. At altars, the blood was sprinkled upon the body; at the Lord's Table, when faith is present, it is sprinkled upon the heart and conscience. And the effect is peace. Being justified by faith we have peace with God through our Lord Jesus Christ. There is no more condemnation for us, than for Christ himself. The sword of justice can find no spot on the believing sinner, which is not covered with the blood of Jesus; and against that blood its edge is powerless.

And in regard to the other point; every renewed soul longs and importunately wrestles for sanctification. It would be a serious error, if we sought it except from the crucified Jesus. It is a current from his heart. The principle of holiness flows from him to us. Sin is nailed to his cross. Virtue comes thence, to draw our feelings heavenward. Our former life is no more; we live anew. "And the life that we now live, we live by faith in the Son of God, who loved us and gave himself for us." Every believer therefore feels the force of this exhortation, at the Lord's Table: "Set your affections on things above, not on things on the earth. For ye are dead, and your life is hid with Christ in God." O brethren, let us continually look to Jesus, for this complete salvation, purchased by his agonies; attested by his wounded side; and symbolized by the sacraments of this day.

VII.

CHRIST BEARING OUR SINS.

CHRIST BEARING OUR SINS.

1 PETER 2 : 24.

"Who his own self bare our sins in his own body
on the tree."

As soon as this text is pronounced, the
hearer is aware that it is not a singular
declaration of Scripture, but one of a very
numerous class. It also speaks a doctrine,
which is woven into the very texture of
our common Christianity; so that he can
scarcely be esteemed other than an infidel,
who denies that Christ died for us. It is
a doctrine also, which enters into the very
vitals of experience, and furnishes the great
resting-place of faith. And, what is especially proper to be observed this day, is
the truth of all others which we are coming to celebrate, at the holy Table. Yet
it must be acknowledged with pain, that it

is more easy to profess it in a form of sound words, than to believe it; and that it has been so altered, and diminished and shorn of its genuine dignity and proportions, that we often need to re-examine its meaning, and reassert the foundations of our faith. This particular doctrine, the most precious of all to the pious soul, has been most vehemently impugned, until we find even professors of orthodox Christianity, yielding to the influence of surrounding error, and gradually surrendering all that is essential in the idea of Atonement.—It was a favourite tenet with the Reformers, and continued long to hold its place in all sound orthodox churches. But in our own day, there is a manifest tendency to explain away its import, and to concede undue force to the objections of opponents. These objections have in many instances been aimed at opinions charged upon us, which we do not hold; at exaggerations, perversions, and even caricatures of the truth: and all the changes have been rung on the terms Imputation, Satisfaction, and Substitution; as if these had been found chargeable with inherent injustice or ab-

surdity. · The very first thing, therefore,
which we should attempt, is to clear away
certain mists, which have been conjured up
around the Scriptural statement.—Let us,
then, in the way of negation, state briefly
what we do *not* mean, by Christ's bearing
our sins.

I.

1. When we assert that Christ bore our
sins, we do not mean that he was a sinner. It is a glorious truth, which shines
bright on the inspired pages, that "in him
was no sin." "He did no sin, neither was
guile found in his mouth." "He was holy,
harmless, undefiled, and separate from sinners." He is by way of eminence, "Jesus
Christ the righteous." Only as such could
he ever have cleared away our guilt. Being born by a miraculous intervention, he
came into the world infinitely exempt from
the leprosy of our race. He was hovered
over by temptation: but there was in him
no original taint, on which temptation could
alight. His nature was human, but not
peccable. He was as pure as the first
Adam, and infinitely more secure. That
"holy thing" which was born of the

Blessed Virgin, was destined never to admit the tarnish of one sinful compliance. Against a life-long tempest of solicitation, that heavenly Will opposed itself, with the resistance of an infallible constancy. In no sense therefore do we maintain, that the Son of God was ever, even for an instant, partaker of our corruptions. He bore our sins, without bearing their power or their pollution. Of their vileness and lawlessness his sacred chaste and lovely soul had no experience. And the allegation is one which we reject as nothing short of calumny.

2. When we say that Christ bore our sins, we do not mean that he suffered pain of conscience. Remorse is the necessary consequence of sin, and part of its punishment. It is involved in the curse of the law, and in the penalty, which is death; and fearfully is it experienced by transgressors. But He who knew no sin, could know no repentance, no contrition, no personal regrets, no anguish of guilty self-accusation. It was a part of the penalty which flowed directly from personal iniquity, and was inseparable from conscience of

the same. In its nature it can be visited only on the personally offending member. The very holiness, the very Divinity of the Redeemer forbade that he should drink this bitter ingredient in the penal cup. He could suffer unto weariness, unto shame, unto fear, unto anguish, unto death—but not unto remorse. Even in Gethsemane, when his soul was exceeding sorrowful, and on the cross, when he pierced heaven with his imploring cry, he could no more suffer compunction of conscience, than he could speak falsehood, or blaspheme. We do, therefore, in the face of our adversaries, protest that the Lord Jesus Christ experienced no pang of conscience.

3. We do not mean, that Christ was at any time personally displeasing to God. He bore the wrath of God, but he bore it representatively. The sinner, as such, is infinitely hateful to the holy God, who abhors and detests every measure of his iniquity: he is under his wrath and curse, and liable to the consequences of his unutterable displeasure. But when the Son of God assumed the place of the sinner, he did not, as we have seen, assume any

of his unholy taint. In his own person, he was infinitely pure; and it was necessary for him so to be, in order to be the Saviour. What he did, in his humiliation, was what God assigned to him to do. When he was made a curse for us, it was because it pleased the Lord to bruise him. He never was more pleasing to God, he never was more righteous, he never was more acceptable and lovely, he never was more intensely and immeasurably fulfilling the will of God, than when he cried *Eli, Eli, lama sabacthani!* If this exclamation has a difficulty, it is a difficulty for the adversaries of substitution: let them explain it. For our part, we hold it to be an awfully mysterious expression of the truth, that at that moment of darkness and earthquake, Jesus Christ was so involved in the consequences of our sin, as to sink under the sense of agony, and to feel the absence of all consoling divine influence. But while angels stooped to look into these things, they might have heard from the invisible throne, the words of infinite complacency: "This is my beloved Son, in whom I am well-pleased!" The all-holy

Jehovah cannot hate holiness, and could not hate his only-begotten Son, in the exercise of the sublimest holiness which the universe has known. We hold fast to the great and precious truth, that never for a single moment was the Mediator displeasing to his Father in heaven.

4. When we say that Christ bore our sins we do not mean that there was any transfer of personal character. Let it be observed, that the chief strength of our opposers lies in this fallacy. They charge us with maintaining a transfer of personal attributes, and moral qualities, and easily triumph over the phantom which they have raised. We, as well as they, hold such a transfer to be impossible and absurd: and (be it declared for the thousandth time) it is no such thing which we mean by the imputation of our sin to Christ. Our sins must ever remain *our sins*, and the sins of no one else, as a matter of fact, as a historical verity, as a personal transaction. As deeds, and as connected with sinful motives and desires, they attach to our own persons, and are to be repented of, and eternally remembered by us

as our own. And, on the other hand, Christ's acts and sufferings, as matter of fact and history, are and cannot but forever be, his own acts and sufferings, and those of no other being in the universe. There is no confounding of personality, nor has such a thing ever been maintained by our theologians, though assiduously and pertinaciously charged, during at least two centuries. We hold indeed an intimate and blessed union between the Head and the members; we hold that our sins were visited on him, and that his righteousness enures to our benefit, but we repudiate all such commingling of personality as this imagined tenet would convey. — Having therefore settled this preliminary and negative part, we are prepared to come more directly to the state of the question, by declaring, positively, what we mean when we assert that *Christ bore our sins:* it is the second branch of the discourse.

II.

1. *The Lord Jesus Christ bore our nature.* It was the all-essential preliminary to his whole work. To be our Head, he be-

came bone of our bone. "The Word was made flesh." It is the greatest and the most precious of mysteries. He passed by the nature of angels, and took the seed of Abraham. It was necessary to his humiliation. Manhood was demanded, in order that he might suffer, since as God he could not suffer. He was made in the likeness of flesh, and appeared in fashion as a man. And in this descent, he took upon him a humanity, which, though sinless, was so far allied to sin as to have all its infirmities, and all its capacities for pain. Never, I suppose, since the creation, was there a human soul or body so capacious of pain, so sensible of distress, so susceptible of the extremes of agony. The "man Christ Jesus" was not the heroic, blissful man of Eden, but one tempted in all points as we are, sin only excepted. It was part of his mediatorial humbling and subjugation, that he was "very man;" and it was a prerequisite to all which followed, that he should be capable of painful endurance and of death. God cannot die; and when the God-man, Jesus Christ died, it was only the human nature, which felt the pang, drank up the suffering, and experienced the dissolution.

2. *Christ actually endured pain.* By pain we include all, whether mental or bod ily, that is opposed to ease and happiness. It was in this way only that he could bear our sins. It was not now and then, that he was so humbled; but all his life long, till his cross. He was a man of sorrows, and acquainted with grief; that is, the fellow, the companion, the familiar of Grief. Sorrow, like a shadow, was always at his side, till he entered into the shadow of death. Time would not allow us to particularize the pains and sorrows of Gethsemane, Jerusalem and Calvary. Every step was marked with tears and blood. Weariness, exhaustion, sighing, shame, exquisite pangs of body, unutterable darkness and anguish of soul, characterized the scene, and filled the cup to the brim. Follow the Son of God, from the table to the garden, from the garden to the high-priest —to Pilate—to Herod—to Golgotha—and you will need no arguments to prove to you that he was a sufferer. Indeed this is one of the points, about which there is

no dispute. Those who even deny his divinity, agree with Christians that he was a great Martyr, and therefore a great sufferer. And all who cleave to the least measure of gospel-truth acknowledge that these sufferings were in some way or other for our benefit, and are included in the meaning of the text, whatever else be excluded. Thus far, therefore, in our journey towards the cross of Christ, our adversaries bear us company: but now our paths begin to diverge: for it must be added

3. *The Lord Jesus Christ suffered for our sins.* It is one of those truths which lie on the very surface of the Scriptures, and which must be twisted into violent metaphor, before it can be robbed of its meaning. To give but a few instances: Is. 53 "He hath borne our griefs, and carried our sorrows." "He was wounded for our transgressions, he was bruised for our iniquities"—Rom. 5 : 6. "Christ died for the ungodly."—1 Cor. 15 : 3. "Christ died for our sins." 1 Thes. 5 : 10. "Who died for us."—Rom. 6 : 10. "In that he died—he died unto sin, once." 1 Pet. 2 : 21. "Christ suffered for us." 3 : 18. "Christ hath once

suffered for sins." 4:1. "Christ hath suffered for us in the flesh."

You know how easily we could multiply similar passages. What we are now to remark in them, is, first, that they declare, that Christ's sufferings were for us, and secondly, that they were for our sins. A friend, a father, a husband, a sister, may suffer, and yet not for us; or these beloved ones may suffer for us, and yet not for our sins. But the suffering of Jesus stands out with this striking peculiarity, that it is always represented as being, not only for our sakes, but for our sins. This has been the concurrent voice of all Christendom which deserves the name. We almost insult the language of the Holy Ghost, to deny it. Ancient and modern believers, the learned student and the unlettered hind, have read the words alike; and the text declares the same humbling yet exalting truth, that he "bare our sins in his own body on the tree." What is true of other sufferings is eminently true of his death. It was the lowest point of descent; it was the last suffering he could endure; it was the greatest suffering; it was that which sinners most dread. The tree, therefore, the cross, is taken as the sum, the representative, the symbol, of all the complicated endurance.

It is hard to conceive how any honest inquirer can turn over even a few pages of the New Testament, without admitting, that (whether that book be true or false) its writers clearly teach that the cause of Christ's sufferings and death was our sins; that but for our sins, he would not have suffered; and that our sins are in some way connected with all his humiliation and all his pain. And thus far, also, we are accompanied by the vast majority of all who have pretended to the Christian name. But the number is perceptibly lessened, or rather suddenly falls off, when we proceed to examine why Christ suffered? what there was in our sins to make him suffer? or what connexion his sufferings have with our sins? And yet this is the very kernel and gist of the whole inquiry. For he might have suffered and even died, in some relation to our sins, far short of what Scriptural expressions bear. For example, he might suffer as an example of virtue.

He might suffer, as a martyr to that truth,
which is to purge our sins. He might
suffer, to afford us a great motive, to affect
our minds, and so aid us in subduing sin.
He might suffer, to show how much he
hated sin. Or, in some vague and general
way, he might suffer, to show to the Universe that sin is a great evil, and that
God abhors it. And, in fact, these have
been the explanations of the great event,
which have been given by numerous theologians, who have borne the Christian name.
There is not one of them, however, which
does not fall far short of the genuine and
precious meaning of the text. Whence, we
proceed to affirm that

4. *Christ bore our sins, in this sense
that he bore the penalty of our sins.* This
is the primary, obvious, and necessary meaning of the words: that which common
readers in all ages have derived from them;
and which has been received without re-
luctance by the mind of universal Christianity. The notion is not recondite, but
one which a child may apprehend. We
were to have been punished: Christ was
punished for us. We were to have died:

Christ died for us. It is the plain signification of the expression often repeated in
Scripture; "Christ died *for* us," that is
died in our stead.

But here the adversary rejoins, that
penalty must always attach to the person;
that he who has sinned must be punished;
and that the suffering of the innocent cannot benefit the guilty. If this were true,
it would at once cut off all our hopes,
and put an end to all proper atonement.
But, blessed be God, it is not true. The
church in all ages has held first, that sin
for its own sake deserves the wrath and
curse of God, and secondly, that to redeem
us from the law, God sent his own Son,
in the likeness of sinful flesh, who in his
own person fulfilled those demands, and
endured that curse in our stead. And this
is so far from violating any of our natural
principles of justice, that it is of all things
most suited to relieve and pacify the afflicted conscience.

The Scriptures represent the penalty as
a debt, which our Surety pays for us.
We are familiar with substitution of this
kind in civil cases, which would not be

true, if such commutation were in itself repugnant to the common sense of justice
among mankind. Ancient history has striking instances of similar substitution in criminal and capital cases. And the reason
why this is not admitted in such cases,
under modern jurisdiction, is not any injustice in the principle. The case, we admit, must be a peculiar one, in which such
a substitution can take place; and if ever
there was a case thus peculiar, in which
the innocent might suffer for the guilty, it
is surely this. To make such suffering allowable, the innocent person must be one,
who has lordship and dominion over his
own life; which men in common life, have
not; but which the Son of God had: "I
lay it down of myself: I have power to
lay it down, and I have power to take it
again." Again, the innocent surety must
assume the place and penalty, of his own
free will: which was eminently and gloriously true of the Lord Jesus. Again, he
must be able to answer all the demands
of the law, for those whom he represented.
Again, he must be able to restore himself
from death: no mere man could do this,

and therefore if such a substitution were to take place in a capital instance, the state would lose a good citizen. Again, the innocent sufferer must ensure the restoration to holiness of those for whom he dies; which no man on earth can secure for a fellow-man; but which the Lord Jesus triumphantly secures for those who are redeemed. In the substitution, then, of this willing, glorious, triumphant surety, there is no injustice, but infinite grace. They object to us that it is incredible that the holy and just God should charge upon Christ the sins of others, and thus make the innocent suffer in the place of the guilty. But let them answer, is it more credible, or more equitable, that the holy and just God should subject the innocent Redeemer to such sufferings, without any such imputation? Christ suffered and died. This is the admitted fact. Now, did he suffer as a surety for the sinner, taking his place? or did he suffer, without being a surety, as an innocent being, by a mere arbitrary infliction? The difficulty appears then to be altogether with the objectors to atonement.—The truth is, all the ancient sacrifices wrote in letters of blood, the word *Substitution*. For what after all, is the idea of sacrifice, but the innocent dying for the guilty? It was an emblem which the feeblest mind might comprehend. There, on the altar, is a spotless lamb—the emblem of innocence. Here am I, a polluted sinner. I lay my right hand on the unblemished victim, and straightway it becomes in type a sinner. I should have died—but now the victim dies—it dies for me—it dies in my place.—It was thus the way was prepared for the Lamb of God, that taketh away the sin of the world. It is not here and there, but everywhere, that the Bible thus represents the method of our salvation. Isaiah 53. " He was wounded for our transgressions, he was bruised for our iniquities, the chastisement of our peace was upon him." v. 6. " The Lord hath laid on him the iniquity of us all:" wherein (to any man who is capable of understanding the words he utters) does this differ from saying ' he hath imputed to him the iniquity of us all?' v. 10. " Thou shalt make his soul an offering for sin." v. 11. " He shall bear their iniquities."

v. 12. " He bare the sin of many." But come to the New Testament. Gal. 3 : 13. " Christ hath redeemed us from the curse of the law, being made a curse for us." Who made him who knew no sin, to be sin for us, that we might be made the righteousness of God in him." It would occupy all our time to cite the passages, where this doctrine is taught in expressions which cannot be mistaken by an unbiassed mind. And we never find unsophisticated persons, as for example, ignorant inquirers, or our own little children, troubled with those difficulties which have made this doctrine a stumbling-block to Jews and philosophers. They see something intelligible and lovely in Christ's coming into our place, and dying for us. Especially when a soul is overwhelmed with a sense of sin, and dread of eternal wrath, this truth is the only thing which can give relief. At such an hour, there is a glory in the revelation, that " when we were yet sinners, Christ died for us "— that he died for us, the just for the unjust, to bring us to God. The victim on the cross is beheld to be the lamb of sacrifice. He suffers what we should have suffered. He bears our sins in his own body on the tree.

5. Finally, *Christ so bore our sins, as to remove from us all their penal consequences, and secure our salvation.* By that suffering, he exhausted the penalty, and discharged the debt. His obedience as surety was superadded, to purchase our title to life; but by his humiliation and death upon the cross, he absolutely canceled all our guilt, removed us from being liable to any measure of the curse of the law; and caused us to stand, in the view of its threatenings as if we had never sinned at all. A proper view of this is needful, in order to a right acceptance of full and sovereign grace. He who believes does in the very moment of believing, become one with Christ, and graciously entitled to all that Christ has purchased for his people. The death of Christ is not merely a transaction which makes our pardon possible, contingent, or even probable: it secures it. It breaks all the penal force of the law. Whatever chastisements, even death itself, may henceforth befall the be-

liever, none of them can befall him in the character of punishment. The sanction of the law will not be demanded twice. It has been accomplished in his substitute; it will not be visited on him. The cup of indignation, which was mingled and awaiting us, was taken into those blessed hands, and utterly exhausted. The Law is therefore as fully and eternally at peace with a justified sinner, as though he had never sinned. And this is the glad news, which first of all brings peace to the soul of a convinced penitent. He beholds the Cross, and sees how God can be just, and yet the justifier of the ungodly that believeth in Jesus. The sword which was descending upon him, has turned aside, and is bathed in the heart's blood of him who knew no sin. It is the sum and substance of the Gospel. Our position this day is the very one for viewing this great transaction; for we are among its emblems. Christ is visibly set forth, crucified, in the midst of us. We are beside the altar, and before us is the bleeding Lamb of propitiation. Among the reflections which befit the place and the occasion, one or two may deserve special notice.

1. When we behold Christ bearing our sins, we should learn to look on sin with shame and horror. O sinner! if there is an argument why you should forsake sin, it is that Christ has died. How intense must that evil be, which demands such a sacrifice! We may be sure, that God, who does nothing without infinite reason, would not consent to expose his only begotten and well-beloved Son to inexpressible torments, if there had been any other way to save the sinner. Here, a full satisfaction is made to divine Justice. For this justice to remain unsatisfied, were the same as for God to deny himself, that is, to be dethroned. For the sinner to satisfy this justice in his own person, were for him to endure the wrath and curse of God, in eternity. And for the Surety to satisfy this justice, it was necessary, that the Son of God should become man, and should endure the curse of the law, as we have seen. Sin is not the trifle, which you suppose. You indulge in it, and will not part from it; you are so in love with it, that you must remain in its embracing arms, days or months or years longer; you post-

pone your repentance—that is you prolong
your rebellion; and when Jesus Christ
himself invites, you turn away, and make
light of it. You make a mock at sin.
But O thoughtless and deluded creature!
Know you not, that this is the viper,
which if indulged, will sting your soul,
fatally and eternally? and consider you not
that it has already stung to death, that
Redeemer, when he met it only in the
way of substitution? Admit the convicting
power of the Cross. Look on Jesus Christ
bearing sin in his own body on the tree.
Ask your ungrateful heart what more he
can do. Shall he descend once more?
Shall he once more be a man of sorrows?
Shall he be crucified again? Alas! were
he crucified before your very eyes, the
hearts which now resist him, might resist
him still. Beloved, but unawakened friends,
I charge you to consider this sacrament as
a message to you, and as urging on you
the love and compassion of a dying Saviour.

2. When we behold Christ bearing our
sins, we should see in it the object of
saving-faith. In all the universe of nature

and grace, this, this is the point for the
eye of a convinced sinner. This is the
centre. "Behold," O condemned, despairing
one, "behold the Lamb of God, that taketh away the sin of the world." Behold
him bearing your sins, in his own body
on the tree. Behold the arm of divine
Vengeance punishing in his person, that
sin which you cannot without horror think
of as punished in your own. From his
cross he cries, "Look unto me, and be ye
saved, all ye ends of the earth." His eye
singles you out, as he dies in sacrifice.
His arms, extended and bleeding, offer pardon to you. Not even in death, is that
gush of love and mercy stanched, which
utters itself in the invitation, "Come unto
me! come unto me!"—I know you sometimes feel your sins as a heavy mountain,
sinking you to hell; like Cain, you are
ready to cry, "My punishment is greater
than I can bear;" ready perhaps, to seek
some hiding-place, and even before the
time to call on rocks and mountains to
cover you. Your terror and anguish are,
it may be, too great for tears, and you
have nothing but a fearful looking-for of

judgment and fiery indignation, which shall
devour the adversary. And these convic-
tions, though increased ten thousand-fold,
can go no whit towards a justifying-righte-
ousness, nor do they make you any better,
or any more fit to receive the grace of
God.—But what! (you cry) "would you
drive me to despair! would you cut away
the last thread which suspends me over
the lake of fire!"

Sinner — you are at the very door of
hope this day.—'But what would you have
me to do?'—Nothing: absolutely nothing,
as matter of Doing: the work is done;
and you behold it, in that bleeding victim.—'How—O how, then, am I to derive
the benefit of this obedience of Christ unto
death?'—By simple acquiescence. "Believe
in the Lord Jesus Christ, and thou shalt
be saved." Look away from yourself.
Cease to probe that rankling, ulcerous, in-
corrigible heart. Look simply and directly
and instantly at one object—at Christ bearing your sin in his own body. Do you
see it? Do you believe it? Do you acknowledge it as a full satisfaction for your
sins? Do you recognize it as freely offer-

ed to you, on the pledge and veracity of God? Do you own it is a right, a good, a desirable way? Do you humble yourself so far as to forsake all righteousness of your own? Do you accept of this righteousness? Do you cast yourself upon it? *Only believe:* all things are possible to him that believeth. O sinner! O chief of sinners! believest thou that Jesus is able to do this? See him crucified to accomplish it, and doubt no more.—If now, thus beholding, you let go your hold on all besides, within you or without you, and venture the whole weight of your everlasting destiny on his satisfactory death, and simple promise—if, in a word, you believe in him—the contract is consummated, and your sins are washed away.

3. When we behold Christ bearing our sins, we have before us the greatest of all motives to personal holiness. He "died for us, that whether we wake or sleep, we should live together with him." When temptation comes in like a tide, cast your eyes to the Cross. Nothing has such virtue against our corruptions. If we are believers, we are crucified with Christ: his inter-

ests are ours; his Spirit is ours. Embrace not that which drove the nails through his sacred hands, and pierced his innocent and loving heart. In every pang and groan and tear of his, and in every drop of his all-precious blood, read an argument against yielding to the tempter. Feel the generous power of the reasoning in the context: "Who his own self bare our sins in his own body on the tree, that we, being dead to sins, should live unto righteousness: by whose stripes ye were healed. For ye were as sheep going astray; but are now returned unto the Shepherd and Bishop of your souls." Sins committed after pardon, are sins under the very cross. They are transgressions against the very sacrifice, and (if any thing can) do crucify the Lord anew. And though it is true that we still sin, and graciously true, that if any man sin, we have an Advocate with the Father; yet it is the height of heinous ingratitude, and a special grieving of the Son and the Spirit, to indulge our evil nature, because there is access to the fountain of pardon. The detestable nature of sin is more apparent in the cross, than in hell itself; and the renewed mind will more readily transgress under the very threatening of torment, than under the blood of a dying Redeemer. This is brought most forcibly to our thoughts, in the ordinance we celebrate, which is a visible epitome of the doctrine under consideration. Here, therefore, beloved, you are at the very place, where you may justly bring forth your remaining corruptions to sacrifice; and where you may slay them before the Lord. The hatred of his righteous soul is against sin; and the demonstration of this is in his dying for it. Take part with your Saviour against your sins, and (as you handle and receive the bread and wine) look up to him for strength to give the fatal blow to those tempers and indulgences which are contrary to his will. Enter into the spirit of this sacrifice, and you will prove by experience, that the doctrine of gracious salvation gives no encouragement to sin. From the cross, you will go down to the world, more steeled than ever, against its temptations.

A tender fear of offending him who loved
you unto death, will make you walk cir-
cumspectly; and in remembrance of past
transgressions, and wounds of the Spirit,
you will offer all you have and are, to
him by whose stripes you were healed.

VIII.

CHRIST'S DEATH, THE CARDINAL DOCTRINE.

CHRIST'S DEATH, THE CARDINAL DOCTRINE.

---

1 COR. 15 : 3.

"For I delivered unto you first of all, that which I also received, how that Christ died for our sins according to the Scriptures."

THE GREAT DOCTRINE OF CHRISTIANITY IS THAT CHRIST DIED FOR OUR SINS.

THE Apostle, in recounting his system states two doctrines, as "the gospel which (says he) I preached unto you." These two doctrines are 1. *Christ's death*, 2. *Christ's resurrection.* We have a memorial of each—of the first in the Eucharist; of the second in the Lord's day. Both are essential and fundamental, and we might (and do) commemorate both this day: but our chief business is with that one which Paul puts first.—'For I delivered unto you first of all, how that Christ, died for our

sins.'—We often ask how an Apostle would
have preached: here we have the way
that Paul preached. We often wonder
what should be put first: here we have
what Paul put first:—Death and Resurrection. This is what he delivered to them:
and he calls it to their minds. He had a
reason for so doing. After being a mis-
sionary to this splendid and fashionable
city, the Paris of Greece, he had pursued
his itinerancy, leaving a large body of persons who had subscribed to the new religion. They were converts, but very ignorant half-Jewish, or half-Gentile. How could
they be otherwise? During his absence,
they fell into excitements, party-divisions
and scandals. It is a childish error to
think the primitive churches were immaculate. Take for example this church, where
Paul labored eighteen months (Acts 18:11);
and where Aquila and the eloquent Apollos seconded him. Was it pure?—No.
There was defect of discipline, (ch. 5) and
they were "puffed up," instead of removing
the criminal from them. The leaven among
them was bitter, malicious and spreading.
They went to law with one another, in

heathen courts. They abused their liberty, by eating flesh which had formed part of Gentile sacrifices. And they went to such excess, in their public meetings for worship, as to desecrate the Lord's Supper, by eating to gluttony and drinking to drunkenness. Amidst these signs of imperfect Christianity there was another: namely, proud division The Apostle was gone—and the glow of pious love was gone—and they were fallen into parties. Persons from the family of a Christian woman, Chloe, brought news of this to Paul. There were Paul's party, Peter's, Apollos', and Christ's! (2:12) Leaders of parties defamed the absent apostle: and undermined the belief of some. Hence the earnestness of Paul in rehearsing what he had taught, as in the text. "Moreover brethren, I declare unto you," my doctrine and your creed.

I. The Doctrine: II. Its Importance.

I.

THE DOCTRINE. CHRIST DIED FOR OUR SINS.

It would be superfluous to go about to show by citation, that wherever the propa-

gators of Christianity went, this was the
doctrine they began with. And a strange
beginning it was, on every human supposi-
tion. What other religion ever began with
making a main point of the death of its
founder? — Suppose we take the hypothe-
sis of those who love to call themselves
liberal and Rational Christians, and who
make Jesus Christ to have been but a
man. How inexplicable have they rendered
the gospel story! Jesus of Nazareth, a
man of Palestine, a Jew, is dead. What a
starting-point ... for a progress which is to
revolutionize the world! True, he has
died: but this is common, is universal, is
human. To die—is the doom of man. Of
all the millions (two only excepted so far
as we know) every individual has died.
No peculiarities in the manner of dying,
will remove this difficulty. Make it as
painful, shameful, and cruel as you may—
it is still but the death of a mortal creature. You have your answer however in
reserve: 'Jesus of Nazareth was an innocent, and holy man, and he was a teacher
and prophet, and martyr.' True, and this
adds immense sympathy and interest to the

event; but does not render it unique, or
in any way explain why the fact should
become the great fact. Innocent and holy
men have died; and prophets have died.
All the prophets, but two, died. Thousands
of blessed teachers have died. The name
of martyr, given to myriads, was given to
them because they died, as witnesses. Isaiah
and Zacharias died, and died by violence.
Apostles and their successors have been put
to cruel deaths. The case has been made
common, by the prevalence of courageous
faith. But none of these have acquired
such a prominence; and if we make the
death of Christ nothing more, we subject
the language and conduct of his early followers to a charge of fanatical exaggera-
tion and enthusiastic phrensy. Why then
is so much stress laid on this first fact of
Christianity, that is that *Christ died?*
Shall we say it is because he died to attest the truth of his teaching? It does
indeed attest the sincerity of his belief;
but others have given the same attestation;
and other things give far greater attestation to the truth, than his death, if this
be viewed only as the death of the great-

est of martyrs. There is no sentence in
the Book which holds up Christ's death
in this light. Often as it is mentioned, it
is never cited as the foundation of the
proof. For any such end, every miracle
was more valid, and above all was the
other great fact—the Resurrection abundantly more cogent. The true answer is,
that Christ died for our sins—*for our sins.*
At this point again we find the corrupters
of Scripture plying all their means, and
tasking all their artifice, to show some way
in which Christ may be said to have
"died for our sins," in consistency with a
Deistical view of the great event. They
tell us, Christ died for our sins, inasmuch
as he died by sinful means—or as he died
to turn us away from sin—or as he would
not have died, unless we had been sinners.
But how frigid is this—and how deroga-
tory to the glow and grandeur of the language in which this one event is singled
out to be revealed! Others—many others
have so died—every teacher of great moral
truths has so died—especially every sted-
fast upholder of truth under deadly persecution has so died. But Christ died for

our sins in a new, singular, and sublime
sense; not merely for men and for sinners, but for their sins. This is explained
by diversity of phrase in other places. He
bare our sins—he was made sin for us—
he was made a curse for us—he is the
propitiation for our sins—he died the just
for the unjust—he redeemed us by his
blood—his blood cleanses from sin—it is
shed for many for the remission of sins—
he gave his life a ransom for many—he
gave his life for the sheep.—Try the di-
minishing and reducing process on these
expressions: torture them to mean no more
than the innocent self-immolation of a witness or a prophet: and you shall find
yourself descending to a violent perversion
which would be scorned and banished, in
any interpretation of any other document
of mankind. Come bravely up to the book;
and either reject it outright with the frank-
ness of unbelief; or, receiving it as true
and authoritative, admit it in that obvious
and inevitable signification, without which
it palters in a double sense, and is unworthy of rational credence. If this New Testament is not a stupendous imposture, or a

childish dream, then Christ died for our sins, in a sense in which no martyr, no prophet, no human being ever died.

Those who were addressed and reasoned with by the early preachers on the basis of the Old Testament (and these were a majority of the first Christians) were prepared to expect an instance of peculiar and bloody death. This expectation had come down from the first altar—from Abel —from the blood of animals—from the perpetual oblation — and from the passover-lamb. It had been increased by the voice of Hebrew prophecy, waxing louder and louder, as the national church grew feebler, and as the fulness of time came on. That Anointed One, the Desire of all nations— was read of, in every synagogue, for centuries, as a suffering and dying personage —to be cut off, but not for himself—to be smitten with the sword — stricken, smitten of God and afflicted — as one on whom God should lay the iniquity of us all— brought as a lamb to the slaughter — cut off out of the land of the living—stricken for the transgression of the people — as One bruised and put to grief by God —

making his soul an offering for sin — bearing iniquities—numbered among transgressors—and pouring out his soul unto death. These were familiar words to the Hebrew: they had been familiar for seven hundred years: and concurring with the emblematic diction of holy rites, they engendered an expectation of death, and of death for sin, and in the room of the sinner. Every morning and evening lamb prepared the way for the proclamation of the Forerunner—Behold the Lamb of God, which taketh away the sin of the world!

When therefore Paul and his fellows announced that the Messiah had come, and had come to die, they announced no new thing; and when they added he died for our sins, they had not an intelligent hearer in Jerusalem or Corinth, who did not understand them to say (whether he believed or not) that this same Jesus had died as a sacrifice for sin.

They addressed themselves to sinners, and called them, as such, to repent; and it was to this character that they declared Christ, as dying, to be suited and welcome. Converts gathered to them — not as eager learners, simply seeking a new scheme of truth, rendered more tender and moving by reason of the teacher's martyrdom; but as polluted creatures in peril of guilt, agonized about the way of escape from a sentence which conscience told them was certain, imminent, and deserved. It is time for us to look at the plain truth: He who with this bible in his hand, would tear from it the piacular death of a divine Redeemer, as a substitute, and a sacrifice for sin—trifles with its serious language —turns its transports into fustian—and its praises into inane hyperbole—unravels the very warp of the texture—and drains away the vital fluid from vein, artery, and heart. Be it true or be it false, it contains in letters of crimson, on every page, this significant and inseparable characteristic, that Christ died for our sins. Of all its objects, that which stands in high relief is the Cross. Of all its syllables, the most sacred is blood. Of all that is rehearsed concerning Messiah, the memorable part is, that he laid down his life. Of all its ordinances, the most striking is that which commemorates a body broken and blood poured out. It is the grand distinction of the book: it is the essence of the gospel. The grand truth of a dying Messiah is the burden of Jewish prophecy; modern Jews, Mohammedans and Infidels reject it. The two last do this with less embarrassment, because they are not troubled with the book of inspiration: the Israelites are more perplexed, because every part of their own Scriptures testifies against them. But most to be pitied of all are those nominal Christians, who have not gone far enough in the liberal school to account the New Testament a mythology, but who nevertheless wink hard to avoid seeing a divine Atonement. It is like ignoring the sun in the heavens. That Christ died, and in no insignificant sense, yea in such a sense as to bring it home to every reader's heart, is the assertion which more than all others recurs in the Christian Scriptures. And it is just as interesting now, to us, and to thousands, as it was eighteen centuries ago, to the disciples. Christ died for our sins. Being God and man, in two natures, but one person, as mediator, he freely offered himself, by his inno-

cent bloodshedding, and cruel ignominious
death, to be a sacrifice of expiation, in the
place of sinful men; and by this act and
this suffering, in our stead, and as our
constituted surety, sponsor, trustee, representative, and Head, he did place himself
under the law, as we were under the law;
and bore its curse and pain and we should
have borne its curse and pain. By this
death, which was the penalty of the law;
he fully and infinitely satisfied God's justice; by reason of the infinite dignity and
value (conferred on pangs which were limited as to time) derived from his godhead.
By this vicarious death, Christ exhausted
the punishment—drank up the cup of vengeance—expunged the debt—washed away
the guilt — and opened heaven to all believers. By this death, for our sins, there
is a pardon offered, on terms of absolute
gratuity. On the part of the recipient as
to merit or legal condition the requirement
is *nothing*. We mean this by a free gospel, and we mean nothing less than this.
It is a free pardon and absolute remission
of the debt; and the belief of this free
grace, in its true divine fulness, is faith.

This is saving faith. Christ died for our
sins, as a fruit of infinite love on the part
of the Father. It is heathenish, it is blasphemous, to represent the adorable Father
as a reluctant Despot, appeased by his
kinder Son. God the Father is the fountain of Deity, and the fountain of grace.
Before there were any worlds this Lamb
was slain in decree. He planned the
scheme of mercy and gave his Son to be
the Saviour of the world. The Father, the
Son and the Holy Ghost, One Jehovah, is
the God into whose name we are baptized; and to this indivisible Unity of the
Godhead, we owe our whole salvation.
When Jesus Christ died upon the cross at
Golgotha, it was not God who died; as a
matter of dissolution and suffering—but the
humanity which died was exalted by the
united deity, and hence the acts and functions of one nature are in common language ascribed to the other. More properly however all atoning acts are ascribed
to the whole mediatorial person—the Messiah — " CHRIST died for our sins." That
event, to which all the old world looks
forward, and to which all the new and

greater world looks back, is the very cause of our redemption; and the fact which we celebrate this day.

II.

The Importance of the Doctrine that Christ died for our sins: the place which it occupies in the Christian system: in other words, why did the Apostle Paul make it the very beginning of his preaching? "I delivered unto you first of all that which I also received, how that Christ died for our sins." Why this prominence, and why did he so earnestly place this singular doctrine in the forefront? Now really the answers to this question must be as numerous, as the topic is vast; but a few, most briefly given, must suffice. Paul began with this:

1. Because it was most struck at by enemies. Though not a blind zealot who courted opposition, and though he knew (no man better) how to become all things to all men; he was no trimmer; and when any known doctrine of his master was impugned, that was the doctrine to which he devoted himself in affectionate defence.

The crucified Nazarene was maligned by Jews, and a laughing-stock to Greeks and Romans: a stumbling-stone, over which Israelites (looking for a temporal prince) blundered and fell into disbelief. It was an unphilosophic crudity, to the learned Athenian, into which he would not deign to look. This was that "offence of the Cross," of which he speaks. This caused the Pharisee' and Sadducee alike to abhor a religion which instead of gratifying their insane national pride by exalting the dynasty of David, showed them a seeming malefactor dying on worse than scaffold or gallows by a gentile punishment under this inscription in Hebrew Greek and Latin — Jesus of Nazareth the King of the Jews. This made Epicureans, Academics and Stoics to wrap about them the philosophic mantle with renewed contempt. It was the relating of this event, ("the preaching of the Cross") which was to the Jews a stumbling-block and to the Greeks foolishness—and therefore it was this which Paul the converted Pharisee, Paul the Roman citizen, Paul the Grecian scholar, bound to him as a decoration and a glory. 'I am ready to preach the gospel to you that are at Rome also: for I am not ashamed of the gospel of Christ.'

2. Because it is the distinguishing doctrine of Christianity. This separates it from all other systems. In Christianity there are many things common to it with Judaism, Mohammedism, and even pure Theism; but here is a characteristic: a discriminative mark: a criterion: *the penal death of its divine founder.* The doctrine was indeed in Judaism, but it was a "fountain sealed:" in Christianity it is a "fountain opened for sin and for uncleanness." It has flowed from the Cross over all Christendom; and even the worst corruptions of the Romish, Greek, and Oriental churches have not entirely removed the sacrifice of Christ from its prominence. And this is the more remarkable, when we consider that no truth in the system is more repugnant to human taste and self-reliance.

3. Because it brings men down to the earth, in a sense of sin, weakness, shame, and danger. The gospel is a remedy. It seeks, not to improve what is sound, but

to cure what is dying. It is a remedy which none accept but such as despair of other help. Christ comes to the incurable. All who ever received the doctrine, in ancient or modern days, received it on their knees, or prostrate on the ground. John the Baptist prepared the furrows by his rugged plow of denunciation; and the early seed-corn was steeped in tears of sorrow. Every true believer comes to take life, freely offered, without his meritorious intervention, from the hands of One who dies the "just for the unjust." He that humbleth himself shall be exalted. He that becomes an infant, enters this kingdom. And so true a test is this doctrine, that thousands believe not, and are damned.

4. Because it is of all doctrines, that which lies nearest the heart of Christian affection. It was uppermost in the heart of Paul; it throbbed in its inmost pulses. It reminds him of what he was: it makes him what he is. "God forbid that I should glory, save in the cross of our Lord Jesus Christ, by whom the world is crucified unto me, and I unto the world." "Who loved me, and gave himself for

me." "Christ Jesus came into the world
to save sinners even the chief!" He has
believed, and therefore has he spoken. Out
of the abundance of the heart, the mouth
of Paul preached Christ's death. It
was burnt into his very person, branding
him as the servant of Christ, and no longer subject to others: "Henceforth let no
man trouble me: for I bear in my body
the marks of the Lord Jesus." If he
preached it at all, he must preach it first
of all; and if he added any thing to the
declaration that his beloved Lord had died
— it must be that he "dieth no more,"
that he rose again — that he ascended —
that he will reign forever.

5. Because it is the precise object of
saving faith. To be saved is the one thing
needful, the one thing for which we need
a gospel. But to be saved, one thing is
necessary—faith. Faith is belief; and the
anxious query is—belief of what?—Answer:
belief of this doctrine. He believes God
propitiated. There are various expressions
for the object of faith; but all come to
this: to believe that Jesus Christ is Messiah — that he is come in the flesh — that

he is the Son of God—all are summed up in this. The man who believes this with a spiritual apprehension of what he believes, is a saved man. He is, in that very act, a justified person. In view of law, his sins are obliterated. In that instant, he is reconciled to God. Justice lifts up the sinner, and finds him marked with the name of the Son of God. The edge of the flaming sword finds no spot not covered by a blood which it dares not penetrate a second time. At this juncture, and in all coming time, the one, distinct, attractive, guiding north-star of the voyaging tempest-beaten soul is CHRIST DYING FOR HIS SINS. His one description is, that he is looking unto Jesus. In his conversion, he is converted to this. In his life, he lives by this. In trials, in sacraments, and in the agony of his own dying, he remembers this one thing, that Christ has died.

6. Because it is the key to all other doctrines. Every system has its leading thread and clew. Christ's sacrificial death is such to Christianity, hence the symbol of Christianity is not the all-seeing eye—the creative hand—the sepulchre—the scep-

tre—but the CROSS. With this, you can explain all; but (as history shows) denying this, you go on till to be consistent you must deny all. Reject a divine Atonement, and what confusion and redoubled darkness have you brought over all other members of the scheme? How can you any longer indicate ages of bloody sacrifice? how can you account for the incarnation? how can you respect the groans of Gethsemane, so unlike the endurance of martys? how can you claim regard for the vehement language of apostles and evangelists? How can you press the importance of faith? how can you sever Christianity from other philosophies? How can you cling to Inspiration? How can you celebrate this ordinance? All these, in fact, one by one, are detached and exploded, till the extremes of liberal or rational Christianity concur with the frontiers of Deism; and Socinians glory that the offence of the Cross has ceased, and Infidel Moslem and Jew have their chief objections removed. So they have; and if we will go one step, and reject the being of God, our catholic embrace may take the Atheist within the pale of a church without mysteries, without revelation, and without Christ. But the stone which the builders rejected has become the head of the corner; and this single truth is the focal point in which all lines converge, and from which there is a distinct vision of a symmetrical plan. The key of theology is the proposition that Christ died for our sins.

7. Because it is the great instrument of conversion. If one had taken his stand at the foot of the tree, when they were taking down the stark cold body of the Redeemer from between the mangled corpses of the malefactors, and had looked forward, he would have exclaimed, 'All hope of propagating his religion is over! if there were nothing else — this scene of matchless discomfiture and shame seals the ruin of the system.' Yet this, *this* is the very event the recital of which (before the end of the generation then born) filled the Roman empire with proselytes. And this not incidentally, not in spite of this encumbrance, but through this doctrine, and by its very means. Wherever Christianity has advanced, and its progress this mo-

ment is gigantic, it has penetrated the heart of warrior, savage and voluptuary, of philosopher, misanthrope, and scholar, of the Roman, the Frank, the Goth, the Hindoo, the Polynesian, the slave—in and by the representation of Christ's dying for our sins. This it is, which has pierced through the tenfold mail of Academic doubt and Rabbinical conceit and prejudice. And to this, we who sit here, own ourselves, in humble, melting subjection to have yielded. For it is the power of God unto salvation to every one that believeth; to the Jew first and also to the Greek. And in persuasion of this, Paul preached it, and preached it *first of all.*

—If then the relative place of the doctrine is fixed by its being assailed—by its being characteristic of Christianity—by its power to humble—by its power to melt the affection—by its power to save, as the very object of faith—and by its power to reform the world; then we may hasten to a conclusion, in the way of inference: since we have shown, (1) what the doctrine is, and (2) what is the importance of the doctrine.—These things enable us to come to a judgment with regard to churches and religious communities; and the criterion suggested is the relative place which they give to the doctrine of Christ's death. In apostolical communions it was obvious, prominent, and far above all mistake or doubt. There it stood, bold and undeniable, not only the main thing, but pervading every part. A company of disciples, among whom high thoughts of the cross and the Redeemer were not common, was without example in that day. Among their faults, that of throwing the principal figure into the back-ground was not one. Beware my brethren of connexion even occasional with societies which sacrifice the great fact of our religion to a pretended Charity. A heart touched with genuine love, will never feel at home in services where the divinity of Christ and his vicarious death are only whispered in elegant generalities, or perhaps sunk in deceitful silence. Be afraid of those circles however tasteful and liberal, where this truth is treated as a mystery too dangerous to handle, or where you are invited to find relief to your souls without a propitiation.

In like manner, we may judge of books, preaching, and systems of theology. Try them by this question: What think ye of Christ? And if they speak double phrases, if they hesitate, if they falter, if they resolve atonement into symbol and metaphor, if they leave you in doubt as to what they mean, if they suffer you to forget the blood of the cross, while they are large on law, obligation, good works, the beauty of virtue, the excellency of man, the perfectibility of the species, and the mercy of God to the finally impenitent—bid them not God speed, and receive them not into your houses. If you would know the camp of an enemy from that of a friend, see well to it, that the standard of the text floats conspicuously. For there are many Antichrists, and Satan changes himself into an angel of light. "Take heed what ye hear," and expose not yourselves and your children to the guardianship of wolves in sheep's clothing. It is Christ our dying Surety, that is the sum and substance of the gospel.

Finally, we may here judge of our own personal religion. Let it be tried by the New Testament. Take this volume, and carefully observe what place is occupied in it by the name of Christ; and what degree of prominency is given to his death. Then apply the rule to the heart, and examine whether the same place and the same prominency are yielded to the suffering Lord in your own experience. Is Jesus Christ a dim, distant light, glimmering through clouds in the horizon of your thoughts; or does he rise upon your heaven like the sun in his strength, and fill the field of vision with his soft effulgence? So far as you are conscious of defect earnestly seek amendment, by contemplation of an atoning Saviour. Aid your faith by the word, and the sacrament. Consider that this one fact is perpetuated by a holy ordinance; and look on the body broken and the blood shed, as the gospel in a sensible form. Behold him—behold him always—'Him first, him last, him midst, and without end!' Then when your time comes, you shall say as dying men have said, 'None but Christ—none but Christ!'

IX.

COMMUNION IN CHRIST'S BODY
AND BLOOD.

COMMUNION IN CHRIST'S BODY
AND BLOOD.

1 CORINTHIANS 10 : 16.

"The cup of blessing which we bless, is it not the communion of the blood of Christ? The bread which we break, is it not the communion of the body of Christ?"

THERE is no part of the Scriptures, in which we have so much concerning the actual celebration of the Lord's Supper, as in this letter of Paul to the converts at Corinth. Nor is there any congregation of primitive days, about which we learn so many details, as this very church. We are admitted to see the good and the evil of their character. The glimpse thus afforded is useful, in correcting that exaggerated estimate which superstition forms, concerning the knowledge and purity of apostolical churches. We see that there were tares among the wheat; and that Corinthian human nature, even under the very chiefest of the apostles, was human nature still. We see that those who sat down at the table of Christ, were no more then, than they are now, unblemished characters. We perceive the society rent by factions, under the several watchwords of Paul, Apollos, Cephas, and even Christ. We observe them going to law, against brethren, before heathen courts; retaining among them voluptuous professors; rashly sitting down at idolatrous banquets; breaking forth into gross indecorum and confusion in assemblies; and almost ready to forsake the apostle, and go after false teachers. But the most painful and mortifying revelation which is made, of their internal condition, relates to their desecration of this holy table. So far had corruption made head among them, that they turned the Lord's Supper into a common feast, and one was hungry and another drunken (11:21). As if they had had no houses to eat and drink in, they ate and drank to repletion in the house of God, and shamed the poor, to whom nothing was remaining. (v. 23)

Distressing as such facts are, they are nevertheless instructive; for they teach us, that a communion of absolute purity, is not to be found, even in primitive Christianity; and they warn us, to take our standard, not from the practice of the most favored churches, but from the precept of the Lord Jesus.

Knowing the great temptations to which those were subject, who had but lately come out of a licentious Gentilism, and who were still surrounded by the provocatives of that soft, insidious system, embodied in every sensible grace of architecture, sculpture, painting, music, and poetry; knowing too, the dimness of the bounding line, which in many cases separated Christian liberty from worldly compliance, the apostle Paul enlarges, with earnestness, on the duty of coming out boldly from the world. In respect, for example, to dainties which had been offered to idols, and which it was the fashion of the day to set before guests—he admits 8 : 4 that 'an idol is nothing'—the image of a non-entity—that the Jove, the Venus, and the Mars, of their statuary, never existed but in the imagination of

superstition and art—and that food however consecrated to these chimeras, could
derive from the ceremony no intrinsic pollution.   Nevertheless, on a principle of
Christian charity, he instructs them not to
touch this food, in cases where it might
be construed into a recognition of the false
god. 8:9 "Take heed, lest this liberty of
yours become a stumbling block to them
that are weak." He urges on them (c. 10)
the high duty of being all for Christ, and
of making a broad separation between
themselves and the world.   And he en-
forces this by what may be called a *sacramental* reason.   v. 21 "Ye cannot drink
the cup of the Lord, and the cup of devils; ye cannot be partakers of the Lord's
table, and of the table of devils."   It is
with this precise intention, and with no
other, that Paul introduces the words of
my text. They are often cited with another
meaning; and taken by themselves they
carry another; but this is their signification in the apostle's train of thought.—
Look carefully at the opening of this tenth
chapter. You will find him arguing from
the Jewish sacraments, which were types

of ours; from the Jewish communion in
these sacraments, which was a type of our
communion; from their sins against this
profession, which are figures of our sins;
and from their punishment, which prefig-
ured our punishment. These ancients (says
he) had their sacraments. Is it baptism?
They were all baptized unto Moses, in the
cloud and in the sea, hovering over them,
sprinkling them, and flowing about them.
Is it the sacred table? They did all eat
the same spiritual meat (manna) and did
all drink the same spiritual drink (the
Rock). They sinned and fell, at least
twenty-three thousand in one day: they
were destroyed of serpents. You are yourselves liable to temptation. It is the human lot. v. 13 It is 'common to man.'
Your present temptation is the surrounding
idolatry of licentious Corinth—(it was the
Paris of ancient luxury). You are prompt-
ed by every social feeling, by every lingering habit, by the seductions of sense and
the blandishments of taste, to go into communion with the Gentile world. I warn
you against such fellowship, and I warn
you by all the sacredness of that other,

higher fellowship, in which you are embraced. I speak as to wise men; judge ye what I say. The cup of blessing which we bless, is it not the communion of the blood of Christ? the bread which we break, is it not the communion of the body of Christ?'—Such is the process of thought by which the apostle is led to the words on which we meditate; and it affords the just clew to their meaning and their application. Let us enter upon this inquiry.

The cases are few, in which any single word in one language, precisely answers to any single word in another language: of this none are so well convinced as accomplished philologists. Between an ancient and a modern tongue, the discrepance must of necessity be more wide. The remark applies to the word *communion*, in the text. It includes the idea of participation, of fellowship, of joint-reception. The "communion of the blood of Christ," is the joint, or common partaking of the blood of Christ. The "communion of the body of Christ," is the joint partaking of the body of Christ. If but a single soul were the recipient of salvation, there is a sense in which he might be said to have communion with Christ's body; and this sense is included; but more is included, namely, that he partakes in common with many others. (v. 2, 3) The Israelites 'were all under the cloud, and all passed through the sea.' And, just after our text, "for we, being many are one loaf, and one body: for we are all partakers of that one loaf." As many grains of wheat, ground and kneaded and compacted, form the unity of a single loaf of bread ... thus many believers, joined to Christ, and joined to each other, form one corporate structure of Christian community. The two leading thoughts are therefore, that believers have communion or participation or fellowship, with Christ; and that, in this, they have fellowship with one another. And this is set forth, by vivid emblem, in the one loaf of the sacrament, and the one cup of blessing.

When the simple article of bread, is disclosed to view, upon the Lord's table, it is meant to be an object of the senses, and should be carefully regarded. It is eminently suggestive of the idea of partici-

pation. It must be partaken of, or it is
nothing. It is bread—the simplest and
most universal means of human nourishment; and thus the basis of human
strength and even life. You need not be
instructed, whom it denotes. "The bread
of God!"—"The bread of God is he who
cometh down from heaven, and giveth life
unto the world." The spiritual sustenance
and nutriment of all who truly live. Let
us cry (more understandingly than those
Jews) 'Lord, evermore give us this bread!'
—Hear the Lord's reply: 'I am the bread
of life: he that cometh to me (a description of faith) shall never hunger; and he
that believeth on me (faith itself) shall
never thirst.'—Here is participation. The
bread is partaken of: and how it is partaken of, is equally clear; it is by coming
to him—that is, by believing on him. As
it is by eating bread, and in no other
way, that we gain any advantage from it;
so it is by coming to Christ—by believing
on Christ—that we derive his spiritual life.
"Verily, verily, I say unto you, He that
believeth on me hath everlasting life; I
am that bread of life. This is the bread

which cometh down from heaven, that a
man may eat thereof and not die. I am
the living bread which came down from
heaven; if any man eat of this bread, he
shall live forever; and the bread which I
will give is my flesh, which I will give
for the life of the world." This brings us
to the very heart of the subject. The
bread signifies the dying Redeemer. This
is my body, broken for you. This gives
meaning to the breaking of the bread:
that sacred body was broken; broken by
years of anticipative dying—broken in the
anguish of the garden; broken by the buf-
fetings of the soldiery and the mob—broken by the Roman scourge, the thongs, the
thorns—broken by the hammer, nails and
spear—broken on the accursed tree—broken
by the awful, unseen, insupportable, almighty, hand of punitive Justice. The loaf is
therefore broken; and as we are to partake of it—and as we have seen that participation is by 'coming,' by 'believing'—it
follows that this faith must have special
reference to the expiatory character of him
to whom we come: the bread which I
give is my flesh, which I give for the life

of the world;' Christ's body, which he lays
upon the altar as a sacrifice. In looking
at the broken bread, we look at Jesus
Christ, as the oblation for our sins.

But the emblem is twofold: and we arrive at the same point by this other path.
'The cup of blessing which we bless, is it
not the communion of the blood of Christ?'
It is the cup of blessing—instituted by him
whose every word was a benediction. 'He
took the cup, and gave thanks, and gave
it to them.' Subordinate ministers, in like
manner, give thanks and implore a blessing. It is already almost blood to the
sight: it is his "blood of the New Covenant, shed for many for the remission of
sins." It is the blood from which comes
our pardon. We are thus brought‑back
again to the lamb of God, the victim of
oblation, and the object of faith. It is
matter of joint-participation, and is received
by believing, and by every partaker who
believes. 'Drink ye all of it.' This reception is the communion of the blood of
Christ. Whether then we regard the loaf
broken, or the wine shed forth, we see before us, the altar, the sacrifice, and the

priest; and learn the method in which Faith participates in the nourishment and the life. Thus we need no longer say with the Jews, 'How can this man give us his flesh to eat?' nor be astounded when we hear the Master's words: 'Except ye eat the flesh of the Son of Man, and drink his blood, ye have no life in you:" .... "for my flesh is meat indeed, and my blood is drink indeed." Nor need we ask for any corporeal presence of the flesh and blood of our Redeemer; especially as it was in explanation of this very saying that our Lord's words were uttered (John 6:63) 'It is the Spirit that quickeneth; the flesh profiteth nothing: the words that I speak unto you, they are spirit, and they are life: but there are some of you that believe not.' It is by believing the words of Christ, that we have communion with him in his body and blood.

Every mode of outward partaking involves this idea; that what we partake is made our own. This is not to be overlooked in the emblem. He who spiritually eats and drinks, in Christ's house, and who thus comes to him, does thereby receive

Christ. To as many as received him, to them gave he authority to become sons of God, even to them which believe on his name. That is, faith receives. Faith makes Christ ours. Every single metaphor or emblem fails, and therefore a diversity must be used. Faith runs and flies to him—looks to him—acknowledges him—embraces him—is wedded to him—leans on him—is joined to him. Every way, and under every varied image, there is participation—communion—Christ is made over to the believer; and if the faith is strong, he can exclaim, Christ is mine!—But this expression has a meaning, after which we should seek. How and in what respect, is Christ given to the believer? Not in his incarnation-body, which some hold; as if, by reception and manducation (such is the phrase) the proper and literal body, under the form and accidents of a wafer, were taken and assimilated. No "the flesh profiteth nothing;" and that hallowed body, "the heavens have received, until the time of the restitution of all things." Not in his personality, Divine and human, as if we were transformed into other beings. Not

by any miracle connected with sacramental
acts, as if they could, by the mere participation convey grace. But by the appropriation which faith makes, of that in
Christ, which is set before us in this
ordinance, and sealed to us by the Holy
Spirit. He is the Lord our Righteousness:
and in this character he is received. Faith
looks upon, accredits, and reposes in, his
satisfactory obedience and atoning death;
beholds the law honoured and justice appeased; sees the emptiness of all human
merit, human effort and human experience;
acquiesces in this way of redemption, by
price, power, and infinite favor; and takes
God at his word, when he offers a gratuitous salvation. In thus acting, faith is
aided by the sensible image, and regards
the elements as tokens from heaven, that
the blessings of the covenant are proffered
and secured. Thus looking away from self,
and from all experience, feeling or qualifi-
cation within, as conscious that these can
never reach the due amount, the believer
looks without, to the finished righteousness
of Jesus Christ; saying in silence, perhaps
in the very moment of partaking, 'This

righteousness, thus freely offered, I a wretch
ed, condemned, helpless, unclean, sinner, do
here take as mine, simply and solely because God, who cannot lie, declares that he
gives it to me in the gospel. That broken
body and shed blood were broken and
shed for the remission of sin; and of this,
these emblems, which I taste and handle,
are the evidences. The offer is to every
one who will come: Lord I come; it is
all I can; receive me in the name of thy
Son!'—This is communion, that is participation, of the body and blood of Christ.
That is, it is the beginning of the fellowship; but it is not the end. There is an
intercourse begun by the weakest and ear-
liest faith, which is kept up, and carried
to higher and more tender connexion, as
light beams more strongly. You have but
moistened your lips at the springing fountain. The crag that was smitten at Horeb
did not more largely satisfy the thirsty
multitude, than the stream of grace from
our Redeemer's opened side revives the
heart of the contrite ones. They drink of
the spiritual Rock that follows them, and
that rock is Christ. "If any man believe

in me, from within him shall flow rivers
of living waters." These wells of salvation
irrigate the desert, and mark all the stages
of the way. Various are the times and
occasions upon which disciples have this
communion with Christ. Over the opened
Bible, where he is the glory of both testa-
ments; on their knees—when they look up
into his face of brotherly compassion; in
the circle of praying brethren, which they
do not learn to neglect until they have
begun to hew other cisterns; in the hon-
ored sanctuary; and above all at the table
of their Master; they hear his voice, saying "Eat O friends! drink, yea drink abundantly, O beloved!" They go from strength
to strength, every one appeareth before
God in Zion. Sometimes the chief fruits
of Christian communion are late in life,
and winter is made to show the blossoms
of spring. So that the barrenness, unfaith-
fulness, and coldness of early profession
give place to the high experience of advanced stages of the divine life. This progress is however of the same nature, greatly
changing in degree and in enjoyment.
Partaking of Christ as his righteousness,

the most fearful and doubting disciple, is henceforth entitled to full remission, and to all the benefits of the Lord's death. Such is therefore the first leading thought of the text, namely, that believers have communion, or participation, or fellowship, with Christ.

II.

The second is like unto it; *that they have fellowship with one another:* "the communion of the body of Christ; the communion of the blood of Christ." It was to the body of disciples, that he said, Take, eat—Drink ye all of it. Here is the idea of number. It is shed for many—for the remission of sins. As in our prayer, we feel ourselves amidst numbers, saying OUR Father, which art in heaven; so in our sacrament, we feel the press of surrounding brethren, and say, Our Lord. The truth is embodied in the very emblem "For we being many are one loaf; for we are all partakers of that one loaf." It is impossible for men to be delivered from a common danger, without some common interest as the result. There is no tie more certain, than that of having suffered together. But there are other reasons for this union; the chief reason being the object to which each one is drawn. There is a common point of attraction. Let a multitude of atoms be drawn from the circumference towards the centre, and they are thereby drawn nearer to one another. You need not be told what is the common centre of the Christian world. To that radiant point all are pressing, by a holy and irresistible impulsion. As when some patriot-leader, beloved by those whom he has delivered, when he appears among them, is the one object of ten thousand eyes; and as the throng gathers inward and is concentered on his single person; compelled to be near one another that they may be more near to him—so the scattered members of the flock of the redeemed, as they urge their way, individually, towards the Chief among ten thousands, find themselves in the same proportion drawn side by side. From different climates, ages, nations, races, and religions, they fly to this centre, as clouds and as doves to their windows. Here is the rallying-point: The root of Jesse stands "as an ensign of the people."

Other distinctions are lost in this communion: "There is neither Jew nor Greek, there is neither bond nor free, there is nei ther male nor female; for ye are all *one in Christ Jesus.*"

Intense love of one and the same object must needs compact men together It is true of the enthusiastic soldiers of a great commander. It is true of the ardent partizans of a political chief. Strangers be fore, they feel themselves clustering around a common banner, and heart responds to heart. O how sad, that the counterpart of this is so hard to find, in the Christian band! What must it not prove, respecting the degree of our common attachment to the Head! Yet it undoubtedly exists, exactly in proportion to the love of the Master. If we love Him, we shall love one another also.

But I apprehend in this communion a more special and distinct reference to the very thing set forth in the sacramental emblem; it is the communion of the body and the blood which save us. Our fellowship is cemented by the atoning righteousness, in which all alike acquiesce as their own. This righteousness is one and indivisible, yet is it wholly made over and sealed, to each individual believer, as truly as if the cross had been erected for him alone. Just as we are forced to believe, of the Divine Omnipresence, that God is present in every point of universal space, and yet (far from being divided) is fully and wholly and divinely present to each alike; so the glorious righteousness of Christ, is available, in all its length and breadth and depth and height to each believer, even the humblest and the most unworthy. One Sun lights the universe. This unity in the object of faith, is uniting in its tenderness, and produces communion, in regard to the very means of redemption. All have come out of ruin. All were sinners. All were convicts. All are set free. All are adopted as sons. All have washed their robes, and made them white in the blood of the Lamb. All eat the same spiritual meat, all drink the same spiritual drink. All are encircling the same bloody tree — sitting at the same table—eating of the same bread—drinking of the same cup. "And all things are of

God, who hath reconciled us to himself in Christ Jesus." The very operation, therefore, of faith, in one common propitiation, tends to the flow and interchange of new and cordial affections among the brethren.

Beyond this, again, there are certain consequences, felt in the renewed soul, as effects of faith in Christ's body and blood, which ensure communion. As those who eat at the same table and breathe the same air, and drink of the same fountain, are subject to the same physical influences — so those who have one faith, one baptism, one God and Father, and one actuating spirit, cannot but be assimilated by this common influence. The truth and unction of the Head passes on to all the members. Various as are the experience and endowments of disciples, they all have one origin; they are all governed by a view of the same bleeding sacrifice. The love of Christ constrains them all. The Spirit of Christ dwells in them all. "There are diversities of operations, but it is the same God which worketh all in all." "For by one Spirit are we all baptized into one body, whether we be Jews or Gentiles, whether we be bond or free; and have been all made to drink into one Spirit." There is a family-likeness in Christ's house. It is beautifully exemplified, when believers of different churches come together; when disciples from remote climes and continents, in differing languages, compare their hearts; when distant ages are brought near, and we find the same faith, love, fears and joys, in Polycarp or Augustine, and in Luther or Payson. It shall one day be more triumphantly manifested, in the mutual gratulations and common thanksgivings, of the " great multitude which no man can number, out of all nations and kindreds and people and tongues, who are to stand before the throne, and before the Lamb, clothed with white robes, and with palms in their hands." All saints, in earth and heaven, by participating in the same sacrifice, are likened to the same model, and rendered members one of another.

To proceed further; if we truly partake in the body and blood of Christ; if our souls feed on him by faith; and if we receive of his Spirit; we shall infallibly be led to brotherly communion by this special influence; to wit, the fruit of the Spirit will be love. Hear how the disciple who lay on Christ's bosom speaks in one breath of the sacrifice and the love: "If we walk in the light, as He is in the light, we have *fellowship* one with another, and the blood of Jesus Christ his Son cleanseth us from all sin." "For this is the message that ye heard from the beginning, that we should love one another." "Beloved if God so loved us, we ought also to love one another."—"He that loveth not his brother, whom he hath seen, how can he love God, whom he hath not seen?" It was the badge of early Christianity: "See how these Christians love one another!" It will shine again, on the renewed Christianity of a better age; in which the brother whom we love, shall not be merely the friend of our own circle—the man with a gold ring in goodly apparel—the professor whose social standing shall excite no fears of losing caste among mercenary and heartless worldlings —but the poorest and the feeblest, who bears the lineaments of the Lord Jesus Christ. Such love springs warmly at the

table of true communion, when we know
no man after the flesh, but give way to
the generous and childlike attachment
which belongs to those who are sprinkled
with the same blood.—We have thus considered the second particular of the text,
that believers have communion with one
another.

The practical deduction which the
apostle makes from these truths is one
which should fix our attention. If so much
is meant by our sacramental profession
of union to Christ and his, then are
we solemnly bound to live as a separate,
a peculiar people, to avoid the world; to
respect weak consciences ; to remove all
stumbling-blocks. It is no sign of love to
Christ, when, with obstinate selfishness, one
who is called a brother, pursues his own
path, in disregard of the example which
he sets his brethren, or the grief he may
cause in their hearts. " All things (v. 23)
are lawful for me, but all things edify
not: let no man seek his own, but every
man another's wealth." The apostle was
more noble, and he was more safe. He
urges the obvious principle, that they who

adhere to any religion, should live accordingly. The Israelites "were baptized unto Moses." The Jews were bound by their sacred vows, v. 18: "Behold Israel after the flesh: are not they which eat of the sacrifices partakers of the altar?" Hence those who sit down with Christ, should not conform to the equivocal customs of the world. Though an idol is but a block, or a stone, or a molten toy—yet "Ye cannot drink the cup of the Lord, and the cup of devils: ye cannot be partakers of the Lord's table, and the table of devils." We are sworn at God's altars. We have taken him as our God, and avowed ourselves to be his people. We are his witnesses. The keen, unsparing eye of the world is upon us. How much is dependant on our purity, our courage, and our affection!

Beloved brethren, while we reject the superstitious mystery, and unscriptural terrors, which have been conjured around this ordinance by priestcraft and deception, and which have made it more like a charm or an incantation than a memorial of dying love; we still claim for it a sacred-

ness unlike any on earth. When we come,
together, to eat of this bread and drink
of this cup, we do show forth the Lord's
death, till he come. Is it not the communion of the body — of the blood of
Christ! If the worshipper who prepared
to enter the typical sanctuary must wash
his body in pure water — how cautiously,
how reverently should we draw near the
place where the appointed emblems set
forth Christ, evidently crucified in the
midst of us! With what holy expectation
should we long for the moment, when Jesus himself shall speak to us, not merely
in accustomed words, but by sensible representations, which tell of his very agony
and death! If we have often approached
with little profit, let us enlarge our desires,
and pray for more near and comprehensive and heart-affecting views of the matchless love. Let us, in humble preparation,
make ready a place to receive him. Let
us scourge the money-changers out of the
temple. Let us bar the door against every
enemy and every rival. Let us purge out
the leaven of malice and wickedness, and
keep the feast with the unleavened bread

of sincerity and truth. Beware of thinking that you have experienced all that religion has to give ; of suspecting that *for you* there are no high attainments in store. Empty the vessel—that it may be replenished with grace. It is *he* who says, " Open thy mouth wide, and I will fill it." Have we lived to this day, *for nothing ?* Shall we cry, with unbelieving Israel—" Is the Lord among us, or not ?" Behold him, in the midst of us, opening the treasure of his promises, and offering the communion of his body. That which is held up in the ordinance, is no other than what we sometimes call the cross. Here, as in a commemorative picture for the view of faith, Behold the Lamb of God, that taketh away the sin of the world ! This is the door to that communion, which you may, as an individual enjoy with him.

But ye are *brethren ;* remember therefore your fellowship in grace. Approach as fellow-heirs of the same promise. Pledge to one another, friendship, fidelity, forgiveness, mutual aid, warm affection, in the participation of a common good. Over the ancient sacrifices, there were feasts of goodwill, fraternity and joy. This (though no sacrifice) is nevertheless a feast. The cup of blessing, which we bless, and which passes from hand to hand, is it not the communion of the blood of Christ, the token and pledge of joint-interest in that expiatory suffering? The bread which we break, — is it not the communion of the body of Christ—broken and disfigured and tortured even to death, for the sins, not of one, but of all? The heart must turn to ice, before it can reject the melting influence. Rely upon it — our strength and efficiency as a church, will be in the exact proportion of one common interest, and brotherly-attachment. Receive ye one another in the Lord, even as Christ hath first received you. Let not our only union be periodical, sacramental, and ceremonial. Let not your love be simply passive, or simply negative. Put forth some active means to brighten the chain which binds us. Bear ye one another's burdens, and so fulfil the law of Christ. Love the brotherhood. Look not every man on his own things, but every man also on the things of others. So live, that this principle of communion in a common Head may leave its mark on all the series of your actions

Those with whom we hope to spend eternity in heaven are such as we should seek out here. Those who are worthy of Christ's fellowship, are worthy of ours. But if, on the other hand, we be so far infatuated by the glare of temporal distinctions, as to seek our chief commerce with the children of this world, because of their worldly attractions, and count these charms more valuable than the likeness of Christ in his humble followers, let us make up our minds for this inevitable result: God will visit us and ours with his frown and his chastisement. Our rewards will be in the communion we have loved. Our branches will wither and show no swelling clusters. Our houses, though frequented by the sons of pleasure, will savour less and less of God. The temper of our families will be taken from the fashion of this world. Our sons will catch the spirit of the unbelieving, and grow up careless if not profane. Our church will dwindle, if not die.—O for the heavenly unction, which shall make the communion of this day, the means of drawing us, first, nearer to the Lord—and then, nearer to one another! Amen.

X.

ALL THINGS BUT LOSS.

ALL THINGS BUT LOSS.

PHIL. 3 : 8.

"Yea doubtless, and I count all things but loss, for the excellency of the knowledge of Christ Jesus my Lord."

WHEN we look at the preceding verses, we see abundant reason why Paul, if any one, might have had 'confidence in the flesh;' or might have felt a complacency in his personal advantages and merits. As to descent and sect, he was a Hebrew of the Hebrews, pertaining to one of the most patriotic and favoured tribes; a Pharisee of the very strictest sort. Those who had known his youth would remember him as having every prerogative which the purest Judaism could boast. As to life and morals, he had been, according to their own standard, not only above reproach but zealous even to enthusiasm and fury. These things, with whatsoever learning, reputation, rank and influence, he may have possessed, were formerly ground of boasting; not only sources of complacency in the sight of men, but cause of confidence in the sight of God. By these covenant-rights, by this title as a son of Abraham, by this adherence to the law of Moses, by this fanatical championship for the old religion, he had hoped to save his soul. But now the current of his thoughts, judgments and affections has been entirely reversed; so that all these advantages he regards as nothing; and this in comparison of a new treasure which he has gained. Like the merchantman, having found the pearl of great price, he sells his all, to buy it. "But what things were gain to me, those I counted loss for Christ. Yea doubtless, and I count all things but loss for the excellency of the knowledge of Christ Jesus my Lord: for whom I have suffered the loss of all things, and do count them but dung, that I may win Christ."

THE TRUE DISCIPLE RECKONS ALL ATTAINMENTS AND ADVANTAGES WORTHLESS, IN COMPARISON WITH THE KNOWLEDGE OF CHRIST.

Expecting to revert to the same topic,

let us here observe, that the peculiar expression "the knowledge of Christ Jesus," has great significancy. It is by knowing Christ, that we come to obtain his grace. It is by knowing, that we believe. That which we believe, to the saving of our souls, is matter of previous knowledge. "This is life eternal, that they might know Thee, the only true God, and Jesus Christ, whom thou hast sent." Jo. 17:3. Mark the expression, the only true God: God is the infinite, eternal, essential Truth. The object of all faith and all knowledge is truth. "God is Light." Jesus is "the true light." The soul's apprehension of this light of truth, embodied in the Lord Christ as in a permanent luminary, is salvation. Thus man is dealt with as a rational creature, an intelligence made to seek and enjoy truth, an immortal spirit destined to be forever conversant with the true light. At the juncture of first believing, the soul comes out of darkness into day, and fixes its gaze upon the Sun of righteousness. "At midday, O King," said Paul to Agrippa, "I saw in the way a light from heaven, above the brightness of the sun, shin-

ing round about me." This was only a
symbol of the light which was hereafter
to guide his way; a super-excellent knowledge, for which he was to account all
things but loss.

1. He reckons all but loss, AS AN OB-
JECT OF PURSUIT. All men have some object of pursuit; and all great, influential
men, have some object which they pursue
intently. Paul was not in his natural state
a man without an aim. The wheels of his
chariot were almost fired with the revolution. Such glimpses as he gives us show
that his youthful career had been one of
ardor and impetuosity. He had sought
science and learning. Though rude in
speech, according to an Attic standard, yet
not, he says, in knowledge. He had read
their poets. He was of a literary capital.
Zeal for learning had carried him to Jerusalem, to the school of Gamaliel, a Phari-
see-professor. In all rabbinical lore he was
deeply versed. The glory of Judaism had
been his aim. He was in arms against the
Church, exceedingly mad, breathing out
threatening and slaughter, thinking he
ought to do many things against the

name of the Lord Jesus; a blasphemer, a
persecutor, injurious. — These statements
make the change more striking. He is
not subdued into lethargy. He has not lost
his velocity or his momentum, but has put
them upon a new line of direction. Still
he pursues; but the object is new. Suddenly beholding charms hitherto all undis-
covered, he abandons the chase of what
just now delighted him, and goes with fer-
vid haste in quest of the excellency of
the knowledge of Christ Jesus his Lord.
Something he knows; but not enough.
Tastes of this fountain do but augment
the thirst for more. Glimpses of that countenance excite desires for more ravishing
acquaintance. He still is true to his spiritual, intellectual nature, and still pants for
knowledge; but in a new field, and of a
new kind, of a new degree, (τo $\upsilon\pi\epsilon\rho\epsilon\chi o\nu$)
supereminent knowledge. All previous ob-
jects of research and endeavor have become distant, faint and uncontrolling, compared with this new object, Christ Jesus.
It is the object known which stimulates
the ardent longing. 'We would see Jesus,'
cried certain Greeks: 'I would know Jesus,'

cries Paul, as yet unsated with his revelations. Nor was he a novice, when he penned these words; yet still, after years of learning and believing, he is seen, as in mid-race, urging his way towards the goal. No look is turned towards the past; all is forgotten, while he strains muscle and sinew in the course. For what is this fleet pursuer running? "that I may win Christ!" v. 8. "that I may know him;" v. 10. "and the power of his resurrection and the fellowship of his sufferings." The language is that of unwearied exertion: "not as though I had already attained — but I follow after." — "I press towards the mark, for the prize of the high-calling of God in Christ Jesus."—The knowledge which Paul covets, and which every disciple seeks, is not speculative but effectual. It appropriates. It makes the object ours. It wins Christ. It causes the soul to be found in Christ. It takes the prize of the high-calling. Where truth is apprehended by Faith, the truth is made ours. Such believing views of Christ unite to him, and make us participants of the new, eternal life which is in him. This gives the *super-*

eminency to such knowledge. Well may
the believer, for this, give up all, and say:
"This one thing I do, forgetting those
things which are behind and reaching
forth unto those things which are before,
I press, *I press* toward the mark." Here
is intensity. Here is revealed the ruling
passion. In his measure, every true believer makes knowledge of Christ his Saviour and union with him, the great, par-
amount, all-absorbing end, for which he
shuts eyes and ears upon all earthly ri-
vals, and runs saying, "This one thing I
do!"

2. He reckons all but loss AS A MERI-
TORIOUS GROUND OF HOPE. Those remarkable advantages which he recites and repu-
diates, had all been pleaded by him, as
the procuring cause of his salvation. To
this day, wherever you find a Jew, you
find one who hopes to secure God's favor
by works of righteousness which he has
done; and O how slavish and burdensome
are the services which the blinded sons
of Jacob impose on themselves! And how
natural the lapse of even Christian communities, into the same will-worship, as we

see in the Church of Rome. Saul of Tar
sus was rich in such merits. "If any other
man thinketh that he hath whereof he
might trust in the flesh—I more." Not a
convert or proselyte, but "circumcised the
eighth day;" not of the half-blood, like
Timothy, but "a Hebrew of the Hebrews;"
not of the schismatic Israel, but "of the
tribe of Benjamin;" not a Sadducean skep-
tic, but "as touching the law, a Pharisee;"
not a lukewarm trimmer, but "concerning
zeal, persecuting the Church;" not an antinomian free-liver, but "as touching the
righteousness which is in the law, blameless." He had observed all from his youth
up; sacrifices, prayers, tithes, fastings, puri-
fications, abstinences. Here was a fund of
merit, which according to any legal standard was worth more than all the riches
of the earth, and made sure his entrance
into heaven. How does he regard it, from
his new point of observation beside the
Cross? "What things were gain to me,
those I counted loss for Christ." The most
contemptuous expressions are employed, to
show his depreciation of all such merits.
He has actually thrown them overboard v.

8 "for whom I have suffered the loss of all things" . . . . and let us observe for what . . . "that I may win Christ, and be found in him, not having mine own righteousness which is of the law, but that which is through the faith of Christ, the righteousness which is of God by faith." My brethren, this is a most important point, to which I beg your undivided attention, while you mark the precise terms of the antithesis. See the things put in contrast: 1. *My own* righteousness, 2. *God's* righteousness—my own righteousness, *which is of the law:* God's righteousness, *which is of faith.* Legal righteousness: gracious righteousness. Righteousness by doing: righteousness by believing. The former he rejects: the latter he seeks after. Here, beloved brethren, we have the whole gospel, the whole plan of salvation. If you are right here, you cannot go wrong in any fundamental point. And if through divine grace you could apprehend this one truth, in a proper and evangelical way, you would go away justified and saved.

Let it be carefully noted, that, as to essentials, the experience of Paul is the experience of all men who are called Their first endeavour is to be saved by a righteousness of their own. It is the instinct of a nature born under the covenant of works. The legal axe, laid at the root of the trees, effects so much as this; it demonstrates the impossibility of keeping the law. Yet the process is long by which sinners arrive at this great conclusion. The state of many awakened persons is precisely that of the Jews as sadly described by Paul, Ro. 10:3. "For they, being ignorant of God's righteousness and going about to establish their own righteousness, have not submitted themselves unto the righteousness of God." The third and fourth chapters of Romans are chiefly employed in battering down this stronghold of self righteousness. But sooner or later, the true convert comes to the conclusion, that the work is all of grace, and that he must receive a salvation already wrought. You may go through the biographies of those who have been remarkable for clear and lively hopes, in all ages of the Church, and you will perceive that they passed through this very crisis. The history of Luther though known to most, deserves citation in this place. There was nothing which the devout young monk would not have done, to obtain God's favor. Every thing that *law* could do, in the way of submission and terror, was already done. Like Paul, he was blameless. Yet he was in despair. "I saw, said he, that I was a great sinner in the sight of God, and I did not think it possible for me to propitiate him by mine own merits." I tortured myself almost to death, to procure peace with God for my troubled heart and agitated conscience; but surrounded with thick darkness, I found peace nowhere." Even after certain gleams of light had broken in, he would say, to his aged friend and guide, Staupitz: "How can I dare believe in the favor of God, so long as there is no real conversion in me? I must be changed, before he will accept me." Staupitz replied, and I beg your consideration of his reply: "There is no real repentance except that which begins with the love of God and of righteousness. What others imagine to be the end and accomplishment of repentance, is on the contrary only its beginning. In order that you may be filled with the love of what is good, you must first be filled with love to God. Love Him who first loved you!"—When afterwards, lying ill from mental anguish, an aged friar tried to make him say from the Creed, 'I believe in the forgiveness of sins;' and added, "Ah, it is God's command that we believe our own sins are forgiven us, for Christ's sake," he experienced immediate delight; and the pious adviser rejoined, "Hear what St. Bernard says in his Discourse on the Annunciation: 'The testimony of the Holy Ghost in thy heart is this, Thy sins are forgiven thee!'" It was from exercises such as these that the great Reformer was led to ascribe such value to the doctrine of Justification by faith alone, without the works of the law; so as to call it the doctrine by which the Church must stand or fall. In the same proportion, he accounted all his former bitter penances, vigils, almsdeeds and mortifications, as less than nothing.—In this house to-day, persons are doubtless found, who are cherishing the same errors, and setting great value on efforts of their own, which they ought, with Paul and Luther, to cast forever behind them. Instead of doing too little, they are doing too much; but it is all in their own strength. What they are striving after, under the false opinion that it is repentance, is some humbling, sorrow, submission, hatred of sin, amendment of life, secret change, which shall make God ready to accept them, and give them a warrant to believe. 'They have not submitted themselves unto the righteousness of God.' All their doings proceed upon an undervaluing of the finished work of Christ, as if He had not done enough. Joyful is the hour, when all this is abandoned, an hour to be remembered even at the gates of death. In 1855, a lovely Christian wife and mother was in the dying struggle, on the banks of the lake of Geneva. Conversing with her husband, a man of great eminence, she reverted to the youthful days when Christ found her. Her own account is very touching: "It was in 1828; she was desirous to be saved, and accordingly read many sermons and communion exercises, in which after the manner of that period much was said about what man has to do, but little about what Christ has already done. In spite of all her efforts, she could not obtain peace of soul, and was wearying herself in vain. . . . 'I was sad and languishing, even amidst the amusements of the world. . . One day, in the spring of 1828, my sisters and I were surprised by a shower, near (Pre-l'Evêque) the house of Mr. Malan. We went in. Mr. Malan asked me if I was a believer; I said Yes. He asked me if I was sure of going to heaven; I said No. Then he announced to me the Gospel, and two expressions above all struck me; one was, *He that hath the Son hath life;* the other, *It is finished.* O, I cried, Jesus does not merely help . . . he saves! the salvation is then complete. I have been mourning that I could not accomplish it; and now I learn that Jesus has accomplished it. What joy!' From that time there was a great change in her heart; to overwhelming sadness succeeded serenity and comfort."*

This is true experience, and it is common. No sooner does the believer's eye fairly open upon the excellency of the knowledge of Christ Jesus his Lord, than he rejects

* Account of Madame Merle's death.

all other modes of pardon and peace. Thus the beggar abandons his rags, when gifted with white raiment. Thus the ship-wrecked mariner forsakes his parting raft, to be received upon some rescuing vessel. All the past, with its imperfections and its cares, is forever thrown into the shade, while the believer exults in the work of his Redeemer.

3. *He reckons all but loss,* FOR THE SAKE OF HIS NEW ACQUISITION AND CAUSE OF GLO-RYING. For time, but especially for eterni-ty, he is enriched. The supremely excellent knowledge of Christ Jesus is his. It is the same with the knowledge of God's love; concerning which our apostle says,—"that ye may be able to comprehend with all saints what is the breadth and length and depth and height, and to know the love of Christ which passeth knowledge." He who has attained to true religion feels that now for the first time he has the elements of true happiness. But possessing true re-ligion is nothing else than possessing Christ, who henceforth dwells in the heart by faith. Thus speaks Paul: "that I may know Him, and the power of his resurrec-

tion, and the fellowship of his sufferings, being made conformable to his death; if by any means I might attain unto the resurrection of the dead." In this world he has assurance and earnest of what his Lord will do for him; but at the second coming, his vile body is to be fashioned like unto Christ's glorious body. Salvation is incomplete in this world. The children of God are troubled, chastened, tempted, separate. They know not one another. The time of the general resurrection is that of the gathering together of all the Church triumphant. Christ will be the centre of the immense circle, the visible Head of the family. Expectation of this, founded on our Lord's grace and righteousness, quickens the joys of him who believes. This is his honour and bliss. "God forbid that I should glory, save in the cross of our Lord Jesus Christ." In former days, he has gloried in other things. He has left them all behind. Christ is all. The knowledge of him infinitely transcends all the discoveries of science and all the charms of letters and art. *To know him*, is the prelibation of heaven. To know him more

fully will be heaven complete. This was
Paul's single passion. It ruled—it bore him
onward, through difficulties and persecu-
tions. As the swift runner in the games
disregarded all the ground passed over,
and counted nothing done, till he touched
the garland, so Paul despised every attainment in comparison with what was to
come. He hears God calling out of heav-
en; he sees God holding forth a reward;
this is his goal; this is the prize of the
high-calling of God in Christ Jesus. Language cannot describe a more ardent press-
ure onwards. He pants, he runs, he stretch-
es forth the hand, he throws off every
weight, in thought he already seizes the
crown.—When a true believer begins to
taste the blessedness of his acquisition and
to comprehend the extent and riches of
what is reserved for him in heaven; all
regrets for the past vanish. Among thousands who have made temporal sacrifices
for Christ's sake, we hear none complain-
ing. Only false disciples long for the leeks,
the onions, and the fleshpots of Egypt. If
this serene complacency in a religious life
seems strange to any, it is to those who

have no idea of what religion is. If there
is any thing over which a rational being
might exult, it is acquaintance and reconciliation with God; it is being on right
terms with the holy and benignant Creator; it is holding filial correspondence with
him whom we had offended by wicked
works. What are learning, power and
wealth to this? Hear the unerring decision
of heaven: "Thus saith Jehovah, Let not
the wise man glory in his wisdom, neither
let the mighty man glory in his might,
let not the rich man glory in his riches:
but let him that glorieth glory in this,
that he understandeth and knoweth me,
that I am the Lord, which exercise loving-
kindness, judgment and righteousness, in the
earth; for in these things do I delight,
saith the Lord." Jer. 9 : 23 Hear the new
testament version of the same: "Yea
doubtless, and I count all things but loss,
for the excellency of the knowledge of
Christ Jesus my Lord."

My Christian brethren, the character
here set forth commends itself to your ap-
proval, however far remote from it your
own may be. It is no neutral, timeserving

character. Those whom we call great men
in history are men of a mighty, and in
general of a single impulse. He who is
drawn in various directions cannot excel.
But when all motives seem to become sub-
servient to one, the effect is constancy, en-
ergy and success. Our modern half-way
religion, running partly one way and partly
another, fearing the Lord and serving one's
own Gods, speaking half the language of
Ashdod, halting between Jehovah and Baal,
bowing to God and Mammon, this is not
the principle which will make martyrs or
convert the world. The true disciple who
struggles up the rocky coast of repentance,
makes it his first business to burn his
boats. He cuts off every possibility of re-
treat. The great future is so bright and
absorbing, that the past goes for nothing.
One thing is needful—one thing he does—
One PERSON, infinite in holy charms, has
won his eye and his heart. Hinder me
not, he exclaims. And as if he had been
nailed to the same cross, and marked with
the same stigmata in hands and feet, he
cries, "Henceforth let no man trouble me,
for I bear in my body the marks of the

Lord Jesus!" Dear brethren, how lamentably we fall short of this concentration of affection and purpose. We know there is such a temper—we have observed it in others; perhaps for short seasons, we have felt it in ourselves. But the fascinations of society, the intoxicating spell of daily business, the alternations of loss and gain, desire and apprehension, the deceitfulness of riches, and the lusts of other things, choke the rising faith and love, and draw us away from this great surrender. It is important for us to know, that that which draws us away from high esteem of Christ, is our idol. Every irreligious plea is fallacious, and none is more so, than the suggestion, that we shall gain in happiness by yielding aught to the world.* Ah! this fell delusion robs God and his service of half our years! O that it were deeply graven on our souls, that the secret of bliss is to give up all—yes to give up all. It is the wholehearted Christianity which rejoices alway. Entire, immediate, unconditional, absolute surrender—that is what we need. If we could pour a river of Lethe over all the past—if we could forget alike the

good and evil, as objects of pursuit or
matter of glorying—if we could in thought
overleap what remains of time, and place
ourselves by an act of transcendant faith
before our coming Lord—and if in correspondence with this we could make sacrifice
of all things in order to be swallowed up
in the glorious ideal of Divine beauty presented by Jesus Christ . . . that would be
happiness, second only to the beatific vision!
What would cares, losses, crosses, pains,
languishings, reproaches, bereavements, mor
tal diseases be to a soul thus captivated
with the excellency of the knowledge of
Immanuel! What would the gaudy shows
of wealth, the world's entertainments, amusements and rewards, be to one thus enriched! Religion thus understood and experienced is a heritage in itself. It makes the
poor rich; it turns the riches of the
wealthy into dust. Great and commanding
faith, to bring things unseen home to us
with a realizing power is what we need.
We should strive for it, and pray for it.
God sometimes causes this treasure, like
molten gold, to flow freely in the furnace
of affliction. Bless those pains amidst which

one walks with you, like unto the Son of God. Have trials held off for a long time? Await them humbly. When they come, the experience will be new and searching and will reveal you to yourself. In that day you will discover that common attainments in grace are not sufficient for the dark and perilous hour. But if you are Christ's, the sun of his grace will rise above your tempestuous horizon, and reveal a new heaven of peace.

A closing reason for seeking this high attainment, is that we shall thereby greatly increase our influence upon unconverted persons around us. Many of them are sagacious to discern that our religion is su perficial and inoperative. And, on the other hand, though they have no love for a strong manifestation of ardent piety, they fear it, and feel its influence. The presence of true godliness, even among careless, infatuated persons, has a power which we are apt to undervalue. When remarkable awakenings take place, one of the most constant proximate causes is *a visible increase of warmth and activity on the part of professing Christians*. Hence such a state

of things is called a revival of religion.
Without this elevation within the church,
no measures however well-chosen or diligently plied are likely to·have much effect.
Let me seriously implore our worldly
friends, not to judge of the power of
Christianity, from what they witness in the
present condition of our churches. There
are vital forces which slumber. If God
speak the word, an army shall start up,
each man endued with strength for great
encounters. Shame on us, brethren, that
we should have to take such apologetic
ground with our unreconciled friends.
Rather should we be able to say, with
Paul (v. 16) "Brethren, be followers together of us." Those who are unconverted
are likely to remain such, until there be a
new manifestation of primitive fervour in
Christians. While we are making few inroads upon the world, the world is making
numerous inroads upon us; carrying away
weak, yielding professors to its seductive
amusements and carnal conformities; sepa-
rating giddy children of the Church from
teachings which harass their conscience;
lessening the aggressive power of the gos-

pel among us; and breaking down barriers
between Christ's flock and the worshippers
of earthly things. All which should lead
us to importunate prayer, that God would
visit us in special mercy. "Wilt thou not
revive us again, that thy people may rejoice in thee!"

XI.

THE MAN CHRIST JESUS.

THE MAN CHRIST JESUS.

1 TIM. 2:5.

"For there is one God, and ONE MEDIATOR BETWEEN GOD AND MEN, THE MAN CHRIST JESUS."

IN the system of divine truth, the humanity of Christ should be as fully considered as his Divinity; and there are seasons when it is important to bring this precious and touching doctrine before the direct gaze of the spiritual understanding. The proper manhood of the Lord Jesus is indispensable to his mediatorial character and work. Let it be however most distinctly noted, in the outset of our discussion, that we are far from asserting that, as Mediator, the adorable Redeemer acts solely as man. The unique constitution of the blessed Saviour offers itself to us as an ineffable union of godhead and humanity in one adorable Person. The two natures are distinct but inseparable, conjoined but not confounded. There is no loss of either, but both are blended in a single personality. The Godhead is fully and forever God; the manhood is purely and unchangeably man. Properly speaking, Divinity is not turned into humanity, nor is manhood so taken up in divinity as to be absorbed and lost: Eternal godhead abides, in unparalleled connexion with genuine, complete and sinless humanity. But the Christ, whom we believe in, love and worship, is everlastingly One. It is not a Divine Person *and* a human person, brought into the state of a twofold being; but the Word made flesh, in one transcendent, inconceivable, but most precious Personality. So that we contemplate, receive, rest in, and commune with the one indivisible Immanuel.—In consequence of which, the acts and sufferings of the Lord Jesus, in the work of our redemption, are to be regarded as proceeding from the one Lord; even while we ascribe part of the work more immediately to one nature, and part to the other. And it is allowable for us to make this distinction, in perfect consistency with the single view of our Mediator as one person. We may properly look sometimes on THE MANHOOD OF CHRIST JESUS, AS HAVING A PECULIAR EXCELLENCE. AND A PECULIAR FITNESS TO THE WANTS OF OUR NATURE. And this is what is now proposed, in examining the words of the Apostle, who sets before us the one Mediator between God and man, the man Christ Jesus.

1. *As men, we need a Mediator who is man, to bring us near to the otherwise inaccessible God.* The Daysman, who shall lay his hand upon both, must be partaker of both natures. Were he not God, he could not ascend to the height of that infinitude, from which sin has made us so remote. But were he not man, we should be left still as far from the supreme Godhead. The High Priest, who for us enters in to the awful splendors of the Holy of Holies, goes, so to speak, from among ourselves. We may venture, through grace, to follow, when He who leads the countless retinue of sons and daughters, himself was born of woman. When Divine Love would save the lost of our race, it is not

sufficient for his condescension .to stand
afar upon the heights of godhead, and
utter decrees of favour. He stoops to our
very condition. He becomes bone of our
bone and flesh of our flesh. He is born,
he passes through infancy, youth and manhood. He assumes our soul, our body, our
infirmities. He lives as men live, and
among his chosen brothers of our race.
He learns the lesson of weariness, want,
pain, grief, groans and tears. He shares
our temptations, involves himself in our
responsibilities, and lives as our example.
He joins in our devotion, and praises and
prays. All this, while, as to his Divinity,
he is in the bosom of the Father. The
Word was with God, the Word was God.
Thus joined to one who has made himself like us, we may ascend even to the
throne. Here is the mystic ladder, which
joins heaven to earth. God is not so distant, when the Son of God is also the
Son of Man. Can we forego the precious-
ness of this sacred truth; and are we not
emboldened in every hope and every
prayer, when Jesus in very flesh and
blood, allows us to touch his hand, even

while he dwells in the central glory of the Godhead?

1. *As offenders, we need a mediator, bearing the nature which has offended.* We are not only men, but sinners; it is man who has incurred wrath; it is by man that the means of recovering favour must be procured. What the inmost soul craves, is that our own humanity may be seen venturing near the throne of insulted Justice. This we attain, when we behold by faith that there is One like unto ourselves, who has right of access. My fears begin to be dissipated, when I regard Jesus, who is very man, carrying up the plea of condemned humanity, in the nature which he has vouchsafed to assume; and who, though not a sinner, has consented to be treated as a sinner, for my sake. Otherwise, relief and pardon would be only the communication of a sovereign, divine decree, and the boon, even if possible, would be cold and distant. But suretyship is a different idea. The infinite descent of God's compassion is to the taking of our very nature. The Sponsor is our own. He has passed through the circle

of our entire humanity. He is an Elder Brother, the nearest of kin, the *Goël* of type,
the Redeemer of the lost inheritance, the
Head of the Family, transacting for his
fellow-men. Still more close is the tie
He is the vital Head, in union with the
whole body, and with each member in
particular. ' For "the Head of every man
is Christ." He can act for offenders, when
he mingles with them, and adopts all that
is theirs, except their personal sinfulness.

3. *We need as Mediator one who, as
man, obeys that Law, which was given to
man.* The human race was originally
formed to glorify God, by perfect conformity to his holy will. The Law was ordained as the standard of that conformity
From this great intention, the race fell, in
the person of the first Adam. It is only
by a second Adam, of nobler powers and
more exalted dignity that the original purpose can be fulfilled. Taking the lead of his
people, and in their name, he became subject to Law, and obeyed it, not merely
as an Example, which he is, in the highest sense, but as a Representative. "When
the fulness of time was come, God sent

forth his Son, made of a woman, made under the Law, to redeem them that were under the law, that we might receive the adoption of sons." It was necessary that this obedience should be rendered in our nature. By a divine nature, it could not be rendered; by any other it would have been unavailable for us. But now we behold the Son of man, as Mediator, standing in our place, and by obedience providing an active righteousness, such as we should forever have failed to render; but which becomes ours by the constitution of grace. And that which Jesus, as the Head of Redeemed humanity, accomplishes of perfect holiness in act, as the spotless model, he will according to the measure of each, accomplish in every one of them, when the work of grace shall be completed in glory, and all saints shall stand around their Lord in the likeness of his perfect excellency.

4. *We require a Mediator, who could endure the suffering due to our sins; and therefore a man.* Here we are brought at once to the central and most tender part of the mediatory work — to humiliation

and the Cross. "He made himself of no reputation, and took upon him the form of a servant, and was made in the likeness of men; and being found in fashion as a man, he humbled himself, and became obedient unto death, even the death of the Cross." It was human groans, and cries, and tears and blood, which were forced from our blessed Saviour in his agony. As the Head and Representative of redeemed humanity, he learned obedience by the things which he suffered. Death, or the separation of soul and body, is peculiarly a human suffering; and this he endured. He died for our sins. He bore the penalty, which was death, as a substitute. The edge of justice pierced him, in his spotless manhood, when he stood in our place. This had been typified by all the dying victims of the tabernacle and temple, which taught in crimson characters, during the Old Testament ages, that "without the shedding of blood there is no remission." Thus the curse was rolled away, by him who became a curse for us. Thus Divine justice was satisfied, by an expiation offered in the human nature, united to the Divine. And there is inexpressible comfort to the wounded conscience, in contemplating a sacrifice of innocent and exalted manhood, united in covenant to our own, and thus opening the way for the further transactions of our great High Priest for us, within the vail of the visible heavens, whither he has now gone, bearing his own peace-speaking blood.

5. *Faith is encouraged, amidst sin and weakness, by seeing one transacting for us, who is himself a Man*, though infinitely exalted above all mere men. The tie is real and sensible. The gulf between the creature and the Creator is bridged over. When otherwise we could hardly dare look towards the sublime heights of Divinity, we are reassured by the invitations of him, who is God incarnate. It is this which is utterly wanting in all systems which exclude the double nature of Christ. The gospel assures us, that since the ascension of our Lord, there is a perpetual presentation of our humanity in his person, before the throne of the infinite Majesty. "He ever liveth to make intercession for us." And though the human nature of

Christ is locally remote from us, being in heaven, yet it is made near, and even present, by the omnipresence of the inseparable divinity. We can therefore look with lively hope, "within the vail, whither the Forerunner is for us entered, even Jesus, made a High Priest forever."

6. *This becomes still more encouraging, when we remember, that the humanity of the Mediator, causes him to excite sympathy towards our human infirmities.* "For we have not a High Priest, which cannot be touched with the feeling of our infirmities, but was in all points tempted like as we are, yet without sin." In our common bodily trials, it is a sensible relief, when we fall in with those who have suffered the same or greater pains. But unspeakably more comforting is it to recognize this experience of weakness and sorrow in him who is mighty to help as well as tender to pity. He was the man of sorrows and acquainted with grief. There is not an affliction of our nature, which has not its response in that human heart which beats within the shrine of deity above. Here opens upon us a field

of precious Christian experience, which some have not entered. The Lord Jesus Christ is very far from them. They reverence, perhaps they love him; but He is not to them the compassionate, the sympathising Jesus of the Evangelists; he who pitied the fainting crowds—he who bent in grief over the dying — he who never rejected a suppliant. They have not discovered in him, "Jesus Christ the same yesterday, to-day and forever." They have not learnt to lean on him as the personal friend, and to pour into his ear the bursting sorrows of the heart. Yet here is the true solace in affliction. For even when we approach the last enemy, and begin to shudder at the pang of dissolution, we may be encouraged and emboldened by the truth, "that as the children are partakers of flesh and blood, he also himself likewise took part of the same, that through death he might destroy him that had the power of death, that is, the devil; and deliver them who through fear of death were all their lifetime subject to bondage."

7. *We have a Mediator, by whom our human nature is raised to its highest ex-*

altation. If treated fully this would engage us in a copious discussion, being one of the most interesting heads of theology. No reflective mind among us can think without a thrill of pleasure upon the perfection of humanity. It is a noble ideal, which has entered alike into the dreams of perfectibilian philosophers, and the more sober visions of Christian philanthropy. In his original creation man was a faultless being, of wonderful capacities; and we know not what height he might have reached, of knowledge, beauty, power and bliss. But the fair image was broken to pieces, almost on issuing from the mould. Still the craving after perfection adheres to the shattered creature. But all the efforts of ages have failed in the blind attempt, and man lives and dies imperfect and miserable. Shall there then never be any realization of this noblest hope? There shall. The Second Adam, the Lord from heaven, has carried up our nature to that elevation which it could never have attained in Eden, or even in glory, without the incarnation. As the Head of the new creation, we see Jesus, not only exalted himself, but exalting his members. They are kings and priests unto God forever. "That in the dispensation of the fulness of times he might gather together in one all things in Christ;" Comprehend, if you can, my brethren, "what is the hope of his calling, and what the riches of the glory of his inheritance in the saints, and what the exceeding greatness of his power to us-ward who believe, according to the working of his mighty power, which he wrought in Christ, when he raised him from the dead, and set him at his own right hand in the heavenly places." Inconceivable is the glory which shall crown redeemed humanity, by its union with the only Mediator, the Man Christ Jesus.

8. It is further our delightful anticipation, that *the Mediator, in our own nature, is to be our final Judge.* This is a blessed hope for poor humanity. I need not recite the numerous passages, which assure us that the Lord Jesus shall come again to judgment, in the glory of the Father, with the holy angels — that he shall sit on the throne of his glory, and that before him

shall be gathered all nations. The awful scene has often occupied your thoughts. But the point on which I would fix your attention, is, that He will then, amidst all the blaze of accompanying Deity, be visibly manifested, as the Son of Man. In the nature which is offended he will judge the offenders. In the nature which he has redeemed and exalted, he will triumphantly absolve and save his chosen. "For the Father judgeth no man, but hath committed all judgment unto the Son." "And hath given him authority to execute judgment also, *because he is the Son of Man.*" In that tremendous hour, it will not be least among the earnests of safety and hope that He who sitteth upon the august tribunal, bears our very nature; nay, that he is our Mediator; that the eye which pierces all hearts was once swimming in tears and death upon the cross, and that the hand which holds the sceptre of irrevocable sway was once nailed to the accursed tree. Amidst the consternation of those who call on rocks and mountains to cover them from the wrath of the Lamb, the humblest believer, catching the first lineaments of that face which he has loved, and now gaining his first true sight of the countenance for which he has longed, will feel the perfect love that casteth out fear, and will exclaim, "This is my Beloved, and this is my friend!"

9. What remains to be said, but that *the Mediator, Christ Jesus, will continue to be the Head of redeemed humanity, through all the increasing bliss and glory of Eternity.* Here it becomes us to use especial caution. It was not necessary for our obtaining pardon and title to life that we should know in its mode and its details, the wonders of the future state. And therefore a sovereign reserve is employed, in what Scripture sparingly reveals of that rest. As if the love of God intended for his frail creature a series of transcendent surprises, for each successive stage of which the soul should be mercifully prepared, as it is born into new states of rapture and exultation. And therefore we know not what place the mediatorship of Christ occupies in the third heaven. But this we know, and have learnt from childhood, that "the only Redeemer of God's elect,

the Lord Jesus Christ, being the eternal
Son of God, became man, and so was and
continueth to be, God and man, in two
distinct natures, and one person—FOREVER."
Here then is our humanity, eternally present in heaven. We know further that he
is seated at the right hand of God, and
that he ever intercedes. But the Scriptures afford glimpses of mediatorial agency,
even beyond this. More of that coming
state was disclosed to the last apostle, the
beloved John, than to any other. In his
apocalyptic visions, he beholds Him on
whose bosom he had reclined, reappearing
in human and in priestly garb — one like
unto the *Son of man*, clothed with a garment down to the foot, and girt about the
breast with a golden girdle." His voice
speaks of humanity and death: "I am he
that liveth, and was dead; and behold I
live for evermore." Admitted more pro-
foundly to behold the worship of heaven,
he describes a sacrificial emblem—"a Lamb,
as it had been slain." We may rest in the
assurance that the expiatory work is not
forgotten there; for hearken to the new
song: "Thou art worthy—for thou wast

slain, and hast redeemed us to God by thy blood, out of every kindred, and tongue and people and nation, and hast made us unto our God kings and priests; and we shall reign on the earth." Even when fixed in their unchangeable possession, the redeemed sons of men will be but finite creatures, and will need a mediation of incarnate love between them and the insufferable fires of unapproachable Deity. Jesus will still be the Head and Representative of his glorified people. And as human nature goes on in its holy development and endless exaltation, who shall say that the union with the mediatory Lord, and with his supreme humanity shall not be felt in a thousand ecstasies of near affection and gracious kindred, such as we are unfit now to conceive. We conclude therefore that the mediatory office of Christ's human nature shall not have expired, when not only our souls shall more resemble his, but when these vile bodies, raised from the dust, and exempted from infirmity, pain and corruption, shall be fashioned like unto his glorious body.—Let us briefly recapitulate our lessons: As men, we need a Mediator who is man, to bring us near to the otherwise inaccessible God; as sinners, one bearing the nature which has offended. We need a Mediator, who as man obeys that law which was given to men;—and who suffers the penalty due to sin.

Amidst weakness and iniquity, Faith is encouraged by seeing one transacting for us, who is himself a man. As man he sympathizes with us in our human infirmities. By such a Mediator, our humanity is raised to its highest exaltation. It is ground of hope, that the Mediator, in our own nature, is to be our judge. And, to crown all, the Lord Jesus will continue to be the Head of ransomed men, through all the bliss of Eternity.

Let us not now, my brethren, rest in the doctrine, but press on to the experience. If you have assented to the things which have been spoken, you have felt that there is a peculiar privilege in having access to God by his incarnate Son. Faith finds grace nearer, when it approaches by Christ's humanity, and enters through the rent vail, that is, his flesh. Mere humanity could offer no sufficient support for myriads of sinners; but *real* humanity, united to godhead, becomes the stay and salvation of all who believe. The great transactions which he engaged in, bearing our flesh and blood, and the great truths comprised in the doctrine of his mediation, are the proper nourishment of the new creature. The appropriation of these, that is of Christ himself, by faith, is compared to the taking of nourishment by food. Those strange words in the 6th chapter of John, surely mean something, even though they mean not what popish superstition would persuade us. And whatsoever they mean, connects itself with the humanity of our Lord Jesus Christ. They tell us of meat (food) enduring unto everlasting life; this is the food of faith. They tell us of "the bread of God—which cometh down from heaven, and giveth life unto the world." This bread is the Lord Jesus, received by faith. "I am the Bread of life," said he; and again, "I am the living bread which came down from heaven; if any man eat of this bread, he shall live forever; and the bread that I will give is my flesh, which I will

give for the life of the world." Is it not
apparent, that the *human nature* of the
Mediator is thus immediately connected
with our salvation? Is it not equally
manifest, that in the ordinance, which we
are met to celebrate, we have communion
with the human as well as divine nature,
of the one Mediator between God and
men, the man Christ Jesus? "This is my
body, broken for you"—"this is my blood
of the New Testament shed for many."
These words—"body and blood" are words
which savour of humanity. It is a human
victim which bleeds and smokes and is
consumed upon the golden altar of the
godhead. There must be an assumed weakness, which was not in divinity, in order
to obedience, suffering and merit. And we
rejoice in every human trait of our beloved Saviour, when we can thus draw
near to him, and own the palpitation of
a heart, which is *ours* at the same time
that it is *God's*. This is just the place,
therefore, where we recognize the precious-
ness of the doctrine of Incarnation. Those
who deny this doctrine, and dignify themselves by names derived from that unity

of God, of which they would fain be the
sole defenders, leave a mighty chasm in
their system. They say much, and so far
as it goes truly of the humanity of Jesus.
They admit his immaculate excellence, dwell
on his perfect example, and celebrate him
as the chief and best of men. But they
abide in the outer court, among Judaic
shadows. The "man Christ Jesus," viewed
as man only, is after all one who stands
on the same level with ourselves. He
does not lift us up to God, as being himself, eternally and coequally the Son of
God. His sufferings have no virtue of
infinite merit, derived from the indwelling
and sustaining divinity; no satisfying righteousness; no expiatory prevalence.

We also plead for the proper and full
humanity of Messiah. But O with what
different emotions do we receive these emblems of death, when we are assured that
the "man Christ Jesus" is also God the
Saviour! In our moments of self-condem-
nation, we know that we cannot approach
the absolute Deity, without this intervention. Then the manhood of Christ assumes
its just place. Then we are certified, that

the race of men has a way of entrance
into the joys of complete redemption;
when our very nature, in its utmost exaltation, goes before, and ventures on covenant
grounds, into the mid effulgence of the in-
comprehensible godhead.   There are moments of despondence, weakness, suffering
and dread, when the tossed soul shrinks
from the tempest of infinite wrath.   Then
the declaration of Isaiah is made good to
our almost shipwrecked hope; that "a man
shall be as a hiding-place from the wind,
and a covert from the tempest:" And the
awful utterances of Zechariah echo from
the sacramental table: "Awake O sword,
against my shepherd, and against *the man*
that is my fellow, saith the Lord of hosts."

Come then, ye who know your weakness, and who fear to draw nigh, because ye are men: come and behold manhood embraced in the mediatorial work.
Though the Table is not an altar, to use
the popish phrase; and though this is not
a sacrifice—we may learn something as to
the mode of approach, from the ancient
rite—for that too was symbolical.   Come
then, as in Old Testament days you would

have come, heavy laden with sin, to the unblemished lamb, laid upon the altar of burnt offering. As you would have laid your hand on the head of the devoted victim, so lay the hand of faith upon the Lamb of God, that taketh away the sin of the world. As you would have presented your person, to be sprinkled with typical blood; so let your heart be sprinkled from an evil conscience by the real expiation. And as you would have retired from the courts of the temple with a sense of absolution, so go down from this solemnity, with a persuasion, that God for Christ's sake, freely pardons all your sins. Say no more that we make little of the humanity of the Mediator. How truly · human are the objects presently to be offered to our minds! Here is Jesus, in our flesh, weak, subject to law, suffering and dying. Here our humanity draws strength and elevation from *his* humanity. Here we find it sealed to us, that as men, we are saved by him who is man. And all in correspondence with the fundamental truth, that our Redeemer is mighty, the Holy One of Israel; the Lord of hosts is his name. Nor need you suspect mistake, if, avoiding all distinctions, you find your faith, love and adoration, going forth to that *One* glorious person; who "was made of the seed of David according to the flesh; and declared to be Son of God with power, according to the Spirit of holiness (or divine nature) by the resurrection from the dead."

XI.

PLENTEOUS REDEMPTION

PLENTEOUS REDEMPTION.

PSALM 130: 7.

——"and with him is plenteous redemption."

AMONG all the beautiful and expressive
figures of speech used in the Scriptures to
express the manner of our deliverance,
there is none more common and none
more touching than that of REDEMPTION.
In ancient times when slavery was continually presented to view as immediately
consequent upon war, when the soldier and
even the commander were repeatedly carried away in chains; when women and
children followed the processions of triumph and then plunged into perpetual ser-
vitude; when families were rent asunder
and dearest friends sometimes held apart

in remote countries; there was a peculiar
freshness in the word Redemption. It told
of ransom to be paid for the freedom of
a beloved kinsman; a father, husband or
son; of buying back—so the word means
—from slavery; of delivering from merci-
less oppression and bodily fear. All the
different methods of deliverance are in a
general way called redemption. There is
the strict and proper ransom or price laid
down, for the purchase of the prisoner.
There is the free and sovereign manumis-
sion, in which the master is the redeemer
by an act of gratuitous emancipation. There
is rescue by the strong hand of power, as
when Abram delivered his friends; a figure often employed concerning God's
mighty interposition. There is the method
of exchange or simple permutation, which
is usual in all wars, and which has some
striking points of analogy with the matter
now before us. Something of all these
methods may be discerned in the redemption of the soul by Jesus Christ; He sets
us free by his sovereignty—he delivers us
by the strong hand—he takes our place
that we may go free. But the radical idea

is undoubtedly that of proper ransom, as when complete satisfaction is made by the payment of a debt. And it is only by this consideration that we come to understand the true method of gospel deliverance.

The condition of fallen man, under his guilt and penalty, at once justifies the application of such a figure. We were conquered and sold under sin, carried away captive and awaiting further pains: we were in misery. We were under God's wrath and bound over to punishment. It was by our fault; and our offence bore the double character of debt and of crime. We were insolvent and could not pay; we were sinners and could not satisfy. We lay in chains, both of justice, holding us for execution, and of moral weakness and perversion, keeping us from all that is good. Death, in its marvellous depth of meaning, temporal, spiritual and eternal, had begun to seize upon us. Corruption and misery—here and hereafter, was what we had to look for.—From all this bondage there is a Deliverer. His deliverance is a ransom, or price paid. He is said to

'redeem them that were under the law;'
as well as to 'redeem us from all iniquity.'
He 'redeemed us from the curse of the
law, being made a curse for us.' He 'redeemed us to God by his blood.' He laid
down his precious blood as the ransom-
price, as of a lamb without spot. We are
'justified through the redemption that is in
Christ.' He is 'made unto us redemption.'
He has obtained for us 'eternal redemption.' Such is the use of the image, and
such the strain of Scripture teaching, upon
this tender and momentous point; all going to show that Redemption imports
nothing less than our deliverance from all
the evils of the fall, by the incarnation
work and sufferings of our only Mediator,
the Lord Jesus Christ. All the redemptions
and all the sacrifices of the old Hebrews
looked to this, and were part of a system
of preparations, training the mind of God's
people to expect and welcome a Deliverer
of this kind. Believers under the Old
Testament did not indeed perceive these
things as clearly as believers under the
New. They saw in the future a Redeemer
and a redemption; but they saw them

dimly. Some were no doubt more favoured than others as to the extent of these views. Some, like Abraham, beheld Christ's day and rejoiced. Some like Isaiah saw Christ's glory and spake of him. Is. 6. John 12. Prophets and Psalmists discovered the reddening dawn, where the great Luminary was one day to arise. Luke 2 : 25. They waited for the consolation of Israel. . . . . In which reason we are justified in giving a New Testament sense to Old Testament expressions, as in the passage now before us. So to interpret them is no more than what we learn, from the apostolic mode of citing and expounding the Law and the Prophets.

In the text, a sin-burdened soul is crying out to God from the uttermost depths of guilt and condemnation. In the hope of forgiveness he waits upon God, and chides himself for despondency. "Let Israel hope in the Lord; for with the Lord there is mercy; and with him is plenteous redemption." This is the single point, upon which we propose to fix our thoughts, the PLENTEOUSNESS OF REDEMPTION, WHICH IS WITH GOD. But here it becomes necessary to look into the exact signification of the term.

The word here rendered PLENTEOUS, is used in the original with much latitude of meaning, to express every variety of largeness, whether of quantity or number. To say then that with God is plenteous redemption, is to say that the redemption which is by Christ Jesus, possesses an unbounded fulness. And it is this riches of grace, which we are now about to contemplate.

I. IT IS PLENTEOUS REDEMPTION, BECAUSE OF THE GREATNESS OF THE RANSOM PAID. When a captive was freed from bondage by payment, the greatness of the sum was a prime consideration, and when this was princely the promptitude and certainty of the deliverance were proportionally marked. "The redemption of their soul," says the Psalmist, "is precious," that is, of great price or value. We were redeemed, not with corruptible things such as silver or gold, but with the blood of Christ. There is plenteousness in the ransom which he has offered. There was nothing in the

universe more valuable than what Jesus
laid at the feet of infinite Justice. The
obedience of the Eternal Son of God, in
the place of sinners was a tribute to the
Divine glory, and a satisfaction to the demands of Law, more vast than could have
been rendered by all creatures. The death
of Christ, as a victim laid on the altar, in
substitution for the sinner, together with
all the agonies of body and soul which
our blessed Saviour endured, constitutes a
sacrificial payment which is inestimable;
and which God cannot refuse. The heart
often needs this as the basis of its confidence. There are times when all fails
within us, till we look heavenward, and
discern the Son of God assuming our
debt, and claiming our deliverance, on the
ground that he has made full restitution.
On this head our views may be allowed
to expand. No terms can exaggerate the
greatness of the Atonement. It is infinite
. . . . as is God the Son, who made it.
There is no limit to its value, as there is
none to the Divine nature. The type fades
away when we compare it with the anti-
type. "By his own blood"—says Paul,

that is by the most costly oblation in the Universe, " Christ entered in once into the holy place, having obtained eternal redemption for us." The blood of bulls and goats could only foreshadow this. The sufficiency of this atonement is plenteous, yea infinite. If any perish it is not because the blood of Jesus had not sufficient value, or because enough of that precious blood was not shed. And this is the great everlasting rock, which underlies the whole structure of the believer's hopes. Christ is worthy.

II. IT IS PLENTEOUS, BECAUSE OF THE WEIGHT AND NUMBER OF THE SORROWS AND PAINS FROM WHICH IT FREES US. The prisonhouse of the captive or the abandoned slave rises before us as the figure. The Scripture instances are numerous, where captivity is associated with suffering and tears. But the bondage of sinners is manifold; not one chain, or one dungeon—but many. These are all so many penalties; they proceed from sin. The troubles of this world, to an unpardoned soul, are but the beginnings of sorrows. All the distresses, maladies and fears of the present

condition are only foretastes. Yet they are
very heavy, and a redemption which delivers from them all, is truly plenteous. It
is no small thing to be rid of all the bit-
terness which belongs to an unregenerate
state even in the present life; especially from the fear of death and of God's
displeasure, the torment of an evil conscience, the anguish resulting from unsub-
dued and conflicting passions, and all the
temporal consequences of sin. But what
are these consequences to those which are
eternal! To discern the latitude and amazing comprehensiveness of our redemption,
we must be able to draw the curtain and
gaze into the eternal future. On this tremendous theme, we would avoid all pro-
fanely curious imaginings and would imitate
the reserve of Scripture. But after all our
reservations, there come to us sounds of
woe and glimpses of horror. Were not
these among our fears, when in the times
of our alienation, we looked forward to
Death and what is after death? to the
waste illimitable periods (unless there be
contradiction in the terms) through which
Eternal retribution expands itself? From

all these we are redeemed. Yes, my brethren, a life of godless anxiety and sorrow—
a subjection to Satan — a death without
hope—a judgment of annihilating exposure
forever—and the torments of the unseen
world — from all these we are delivered
by the redemption which is in Christ
Jesus. And that which frees us forever
from all pain, in its ten thousand times
ten thousand shapes, may well be named
"plenteous redemption."

III. It is plenteous because it introduces to all the abundance of inconceivable good. It were something to be
set free from yokes and bonds and the
prisonhouse of the cruel taskmaster. It is
more to be admitted to the palace, the
home, the heart, of an infinite friend. How
shall I dare to open such a prospect or
expatiate upon a field so wide! All that
is good in earth and heaven is before us—
all purchased by the plenteous ransom-price.
When God saves, it is in a way like himself. He is not content to pardon—he justifies—he endows with right to life. The
Son is not only seen afar off, and met, and

admitted; he is kissed, clothed, beautified and feasted. The Bride, the Lamb's wife is not merely freed from the cords and humiliations and duress of her long captivity; she is decked with jewels, and installed in all the royalties of her Divine Husband. The slave is lifted to a throne. She who was wooed by the Son, and who loved and chose him in his low estate, is openly acknowledged on the throne before all worlds, as she for whom he died. The blessings of the present Christian life are plentiful; but they are only the clusters of Eshcol, and not the vintage. Here, even on this side the river, are there the joys of pardon, the spirit of adoption, in many the assurance of God's love, power over the world, perseverance in grace, the gradual but certain augmentation of inward holiness, the ripe fruits of knowledge, the heavenly wine of communion, the delights of devotion, the lifting up of soul in psalmody and praise, the fellowship of mutual love, the antepast of glory, and the serene departure to full emancipation. And then, on the other side, angelic welcome, triumph in the Judgment, the sight of the Son of man in his glory, acquittal by his voice, a place at his right hand, a seat on his throne, an eternal vision of his infinite and divine beauty. For this, and unto this, we are redeemed; and is it not then, plenteous redemption?

IV. IT IS PLENTEOUS, BECAUSE OF ITS ENDURING NATURE. This fountain flows forever. Great benefits become small, if they abruptly terminate. Small blessings seem vast, if extended to eternal permanence. But here is a good, intrinsically great, yet running on forever and ever. We have already found in Scripture that the blessing is called "eternal redemption," and this is plenteous indeed. When we shall have set sail upon that ocean which has no further shore, upon that blessed voyage which has no return, we shall look back upon the sum of all joys of all creatures during the moment of what we call time—as utterly insignificant in comparison. Between finite and infinite there can be no proportion. When ages, equalling the aggregate of all sidereal measures, shall have run out, Eternity will be in its early beginnings. No waste shall ever diminish the riches of heaven. Every moment of its high enjoyment will refer itself to the great original price. Among the countless throng of them that are saved, each will look back with wonder and thanks to the work of Calvary; and each new revolution of bliss will only serve to reveal new values in the redeeming price which was laid down by Immanuel. Of a sinless Eternity with Christ, we had better not attempt to speak; for not only words, but conceptions fail us. Yet our knowledge, faint and mostly negative as it is, is enough to show us that the stores of grace are boundless. Can such celestial glories be for creatures sullied with multitudinous sins, any one of which cries to heaven for vengeance? We answer

V. IT IS PLENTEOUS REDEMPTION, BECAUSE ITS ABUNDANT FULNESS REACHES TO THE REMISSION OF ALL SINS, HOWEVER INTENSE OR MULTIPLIED. Here is the hope of the prodigal. See our context: "he shall redeem Israel from *all* his iniquities." But for this, redemption would not deserve the

name. It is sin, which caused captivity;
and sin must be expiated, before there can
be emancipation. This was the reason, why
the great redemptive act stands before us
in colors of blood. The call is loud and
significant: "though your sins be as scarlet
they shall be as white as snow, though
they be red like crimson they shall be as
wool." From all his iniquities! It is the
word of God which tells us, that the "blood
of Jesus Christ his Son cleanseth from all
sin." The blotting out of guilt is absolute
and has no exception: "their sins and
their iniquities will I remember no more."
In their penal quality, they are as though
they had never been. The debt is paid.
Christ has assumed all our liabilities. They
are no longer reckoned against us. "He
hath redeemed us from the curse of the
law, being made a curse for us." It is
this completeness of redemption, surg-
ing over all the mountains of our sins,
which magnifies the grace of the Gospel.
This infinite fulness reaches all sins, the
greater as well as the less, covering and
removing all the guilt of each. Look back
over one single lifetime—your own—and

see what remission means! Meditate on
(for you cannot survey) that lifetime of
sinning which spreads its lengthened line
back, back to the very origin of moral
action. ·The current of act and word and
feeling and thought has had its character
for good or evil in each particular wave.
Individual sins have been forgotten; thousands have been forgotten. Yet oblivion
has not blotted out the record or washed
away the guilt. Your memory of these
transgressions and omissions is perhaps dim;
but your accountability for each is as fresh
and perfect as if it had this instant issued
from your volition. Among the huge in-
discriminate tumble of waves which dash
in as breakers upon the shore of thought,
you may recall here and there one of
extraordinary violence. "But who can understand his errors"—his secret faults—his
presumptuous sins! The more we gaze
upon them, the more numerous do they
seem; as the stars, when one begins to
count them up. It is a sense of this extraordinary number of sins, each possessing
its separate turpitude, which, at the time
of genuine awakening, leads to fearful con-

viction; while the soul stands aghast and cries, "If thou Lord shouldst mark iniquity, O Lord, who could stand?" This it is which makes pardon hard to be believed. And all through the Christian's life, it is the recollection of innumerable iniquities, which humbles the soul in the dust, preventing its ever daring to look up into the face of Infinite Purity with any feeling of complacency. Now all these long continued and multiplied sins are forever covered and removed as to their guilt by the fulness of redemption. No single sin remains unforgiven; for if there were such, it would cut off all hope.—Now as this is true in regard to any given sinner and his offences, so it is true of all manner of sins, even the most atrocious, if only they be brought to the fount of healing. The unpardonable sin itself, we hold to be such, only because (by its very nature) it is not so brought. Could so impossible a thing be conceived, as that it should be so brought, it would be forgiven. "All manner of sin and blasphemy shall be forgiven unto men." Final impenitence destroys, simply because it is a final rejection of

redemption. The redemption itself is good,
for all sins, even the greatest. "This is a
faithful saying &c." When, under the agonies of remorse, a sinner near despair
thinks none have ever sinned as he has
sinned, and declares that he is too vile to
be forgiven (and little as hardened hearts
conceive of such compunction or fear, the
experience is not uncommon) in so saying
he betrays total ignorance of the value of
Christ's blood, and the sovereign fulness of
his grace. There are but two classes of
souls, and two conditions; those that are
saved and those that are lost: "he that
believeth shall be saved—he that believeth
not shall be damned."—This abundance of
redemption spreads its stores for all sinners. There is no one within the sound
of the gospel who is excluded. As, according to what has been said, the ransom-
price is infinite, so the offer is infinite.
Our commission runs thus: 'Go ye into
all the world—with this good news to
every creature.' Every creature then is
comprehended within the arms of the offer
and the possibility of salvation. There is
no need for Christ to die again—to make

redemption accessible to more thousands, even of those who shall eventually perish; nor any need of a new gospel-offer, if all the world should be saved. We need nothing ampler, we can conceive of nothing wider, than the tender mercies of our God, "for with him is plenteous redemption." If this could be brought home to thee, poor lingering sinner, it would be this hour the salvation of thy soul.

VI. Finally, THIS IS PLENTEOUS REDEMPTION, BECAUSE OF THE FREENESS OF THE OFFER. We call that a plentiful feast, where the provisions are not only abundant, but offered to all comers, and for nothing. Such is the gospel—such is grace, by its very name, gratuity. "Grace," says Rutherford, "is mercy given for nothing." He that annexes any price, however small, vacates the covenant of its grace. Price has indeed been paid, perfect amends have been made to Divine Justice, but by the Lamb of God, and not by the sinner. "Ho, every one that thirsteth, come ye to the waters, and he that hath no money, come ye, buy wine and milk without money

and without price." It was the Law,
which made meritorious conditions, the
Gospel is a free offer, which becomes available on simple believing. The righteousness by which we are justified, is not something which we work out, but something
bestowed on us as a gift. It addresses
all transgressors, however vile, in a mass,
with words of cheering. "For all have
sinned, and come short of the glory of
God; being justified freely by his grace
through the redemption that is in Christ
Jesus," the plenteous redemption. Christ's
perfect righteousness, as a resplendent robe,
is hung out from heaven, for the free acceptance of all sinners under the gospel.
And it is given—not to him who works
most faithfully, according to legal rule,
"but to him that worketh not, but believeth on Him that justifieth the ungodly." Rom. 4 : 5. It does indeed seem a
great thing to the believing sinner, for
such magnitude and multitude of sins to
be forgiven without his personal reparation, but when his eyes fix on the person
and work of Christ, he sees how it can
be accomplished, and understands how the

greatest honour he can confer on God is
to be saved by God's method, " to the
praise of the glory of his grace, wherein
he hath made us accepted in the Beloved."
Having reached this point, he staggers not
at the promise of God through unbelief;
but is "strong in faith, giving glory to
God." There is no presumption in so believing; for it is only taking God at his
word, accrediting his promise, honouring
his attributes, and glorifying his Son. It
was this doctrine of free justification by
the righteousness of Christ, imputed to us,
and received by faith, which, when revealed
to Luther, rose on his soul like a sun in
the heavens. It was the germinating principle of all the Reformation doctrine. It
is this day, what Luther called it, *articu-
lus stantis aut cadentis ecclesiæ*. Where it
is held firmly, preached and believed, there
strong and cheerful piety, justly named
evangelical, is found to prevail. Where it
is denied, or corrupted, or curtailed, error
after error creeps in, and the cordial essence of the gospel is forever lost. On
no one point do faithful ministers of the
gospel more feel their own weakness, than

when they argue and plead with a convinced sinner, in behalf of the freeness of salvation. Clear as it is in the Word, it is all dark to the condemned soul. No reasoning, no citation, no rehearsal of cases, no asseverations, no entreaties, can move him an inch from the self-righteous shoal on which he is stranded, or dispossess him of the prejudice that he must fulfil some condition before he comes to Christ. Here the preacher or teacher sits down discomfited if not dismayed. But then, on the other hand, at no one point does the same guide of souls more recognise and adore the illuminating Spirit of God, than when he sees all this made clear, sometimes in the twinkling of an eye, to the hitherto unbelieving mind. The blind man looks up into the face of his Saviour! He beholds him able — and as willing as able. He falls at his feet, without waiting for terms or conditions. Free, full, sovereign grace, abounding to the chief of sinners, has overcome every scruple. He knows and feels that he can be saved; not in consequence of changes of which he is conscious within himself — but simply on the ground of *God's uttered promise*, which he accepts. I will not say, he ventures on it; there is no peradventure in the case. His language is, "Let God be true and every man a liar;" or with our Psalmist, "Let Israel hope in the Lord: for with the Lord there is mercy, and with him is plenteous redemption."

Nothing, my brethren, but infinite love could be the fountain-head of so immeasurable a blessing. It sprang in the eternal heart of God, and flowed out in the Incarnation. The multitude, the copiousness of Divine grace and mercy must be sought in the person of the Lord Jesus. God is love; yea rather, speaking now of God manifest, Christ is Love. And although all his history is one display of saving benevolence, we behold its concentration in his Cross and passion. The Atonement by sacrifice it is, which reveals to us the greatness of divine compassions. As he hangs on the accursed tree, in his last moments, between two malefactors already dead, he exhibits to us the token of cleansing. — "One of the soldiers with a spear pierced his side, and forthwith came there out blood and water. And he that saw it bare record, and his record is true: and he knoweth that he saith true, that ye might believe." That, concerning which the Beloved Disciple testifies, is the double fount of plenteous redemption. Brethren and sisters, we are gathering around the same open side and flowing heart, which left indelible impression on John. Here is expiation, to remove the debt, liability or guilt of sin: here is cleansing, to take away its power, stain and indwelling pollution. Many years after, the same John, remembering the same pierced side, thus writes, (5 : 6 :) "This is he that came by water and blood, even JESUS CHRIST; not by water only, but by water and blood." And he adds, "There are three that bear witness in earth, the spirit, and the water, and the blood, and these three agree in one." The same abundance of grace is witnessed by our commemorative ordinance. Here the sacred side of Jesus is pierced in emblem; the body is sacramentally broken, the blood is sacramentally spilt. "This cup," saith He, "is the New Testament in my blood, shed for many for the remission of sins." The Covenant of Grace, sealed by this ordinance, tenders and exhibits the plenteous redemption. We are vile—but divine love is infinite, and divine pardons are sure, to every one that believeth. Though like David you cry out of the depths, unable to answer for your iniquities, yet you can say, beholding these pledges, "I wait for the Lord, my soul doth wait, and on his word do I hope. My soul waiteth for the Lord more than they that watch for the morning, I say, more than they that watch for the morning." (5, 6.)

XII.

CHRIST'S CROSS AND CROWN.

CHRIST'S CROSS AND CROWN.

REVELATION 19 : 12, 13.

"His eyes were as a flame of fire, and on his head were many crowns; and he had a name written that no man knew, but he himself. And he was clothed with a vesture dipped in blood: and his name is called the Word of God."

1. THERE is a day coming, when in consideration of Christ's bloodshedding and death he shall triumph and reign with his beloved church. The book of the Apocalypse is chiefly concerned in the great warfare and victory of the glorious future, and yet have you not observed, my brethren, how often in this gorgeous panorama of prophetic imagery, there are brought out fully into view some tokens and signal remembrances of the humiliation and atonement? In the very crown we are made to see the cross, and are re-

minded that it is because he made himself of no reputation, that "God hath highly exalted him?" Early in the book, (1 : 5,) the ascription is to "him that loved us and washed us from our sins in his own blood, and hath made us kings and priests:" here is both the humiliation and the exaltation. Again (5 : 6) John beholds, and "lo, in the midst of the throne, and of the four living ones, and in the midst of the elders, stood a lamb as it had been slain." Here is the propitiation enthroned in the very heart and central spot of heaven : blood upon the very throne; the cross and the crown.

The song of the living ones and elders, prostrate, with harps and odors (5 : 8) is, "thou wast slain, and hast redeemed us to God by thy blood—and we shall reign on the earth:" here again suffering and glory. And then the praise is caught up by all creatures, "unto him that sitteth upon the throne, and unto the Lamb, forever and ever." The throng in white robes (7 : 13) serving God day and night before the throne, are such as "have washed their robes and made them white in the blood of the Lamb." The brethren who are victorious over Satan (12 : 11) are said to overcome him by the blood of the Lamb." It is the Lamb, (14 : 1,) who stands on Mount Sion, with one hundred forty and four thousand, having his Father's name written in their foreheads. The spirit of all these declarations is the same. The Mercy-seat is not forgotten in the latter glory, but the ark of the covenant reappears in heaven. Jesus can agonize no more; he can be arrested no more; no more can his garments be rent from him, to be replaced by the mockery of purple, diadem and sceptre; no more can he be slapped ($\rho\alpha\pi\iota\zeta\omega$) in the face, hoodwinked and spit upon; no more can he be torn with Roman scourges, and nailed to the cursed cross. No pang does he carry to heaven. Yet, in heaven, he is other than he would have been, but for the garden, the pretorium and "the place of a skull." There, amidst his loved and redeemed ones, amidst a multitude of the heavenly host, on the supreme throne, Christ still bears the tokens of a sacrificial death; and even when he comes up to victory and vengeance, he is red in his apparel, and his "garments like him that treadeth in the winefat." (Is. 63: 2.) No eye shall look upon the BELOVED in paradise, without recognising him as the Man of Sorrows, and the familiar of grief. (Is. 53.)

2. Christ's triumph and reign are in consideration of his death. One is the purchase of the other. He "became obedient unto death, even the death of the cross; wherefore also God hath highly exalted him, and given him a name which is above every name." (Phil. 2: 9.) Such was the engagement before all worlds. "When his soul shall make an offering for sin, he shall see his seed—because he hath poured out his soul unto death — *therefore*, says Jehovah, I will divide him a portion with the great, and he shall divide the spoil with the strong." (Is. 53.) It is because he suffered, that he reigns. That suffering was penal and vicarious. It could not otherwise have fallen on him. The suffering was for others: the recompense also is for others. Christ reigns and rejoices in his people. They accompany his triumphal progress and share in his throne.

It is because of this that he comes even to the marriage supper, with a vesture dipped in blood. The mediatorial exaltation of Jesus Christ is all in consequence of his mediatorial humiliation: and this is one reason why we rejoice and exult in his bliss and glory, because it is the fruit of his agony. The honor done to God's justice, by Christ's death, is the cause of jubilee in heaven. It is this only which has bought back the body of disciples from hell. The whole mystery of redemption is in these words, which are this day translated into the language of bread and wine, Christ hath died.

3. It is the blood and dying of Jesus Christ which subdues the believing soul in order to the eventual triumph. Of all those multitudes, every one came in the same way. Each yielded at the cross. He could brave Sinai; but there was that on Calvary, which unmanned him, and he yielded to triumphant Love. When a soul believes, that single act cuts it off from ten thousand things at once, and joins it to Christ. "This is the victory that overcometh the world, even our faith." What is faith, but a reception of this bleeding

atonement? Faith looks on, and goes out to, this very dying. Here is the sublime moral influence of the Cross. Besides silencing all the batteries of divine justice, and procuring pardon of sin, it subdues that soul, by the infinite weight of Christ's love—"which passeth knowledge." Before Messiah conquers the earth and the universe; before he rules them with a rod of iron and treadeth the "winepress of the fierceness and wrath of God;" before the doxology, "Alleluia, for the Lord God omnipotent reigneth"—there is a private work to be wrought on each individual soul, and this by the cross of Jesus Christ. Beholding this mighty love of God, the sinner melts and yields and weeps and is forgiven. When the Lord sues, by his pierced hands and crimson apparel, he cannot be denied. This winning of the soul is in the day of first love and espousals on earth. But it all makes way for the lofty scene set before us in the context: this hour is that of consummate union: "for the marriage of the Lamb is come, and his wife hath made herself ready." (v. 7.) O brethren! the day is coming when we shall be among "a great multitude which no man could number, of all nations and kindreds and people and tongues, before the throne and before the Lamb, clothed with white robes and palms in their hands;" but not one, who does not ascribe the conquest of his mind and heart to the believing view of a dying Christ. This is "the excellency of the knowledge." The love of Christ constraineth them. It is a fit preparation for eventual universal dominion, that first of all Christ subdues his people unto him by the blood of his cross.

4. *It is in Christ's character of dying Saviour, that the church universal regards him, even in heaven.* In his triumphal retinue there is not one, whose eye is not fixed on the vesture of blood. It is not the manger or the sepulchre, that we think of in connexion with the name Jesus, so much as the CROSS. See, in the Apostles' Creed, how soon we go from Bethlehem to Calvary, "born of the Virgin Mary —suffered under Pontius Pilate." It is one of the tokens of declining religion when this character of the Son of God, is thrown

into the obscurity of the back-ground, even though much be said of his teaching and his example. It is an evil symptom when congregations begin to complain that they have too much of blood and atonement; and it is usually a precursor of Unitarian infidelity, when the Lord's Supper is emptied of its reference to propitiation, and instead of being a memorial and seal of the bloody covenant and sacrificial death, becomes only a solemn way of joining the church or taking a Christian vow. As in our effectual calling and first believing, it is the dying Jesus who fills the whole heaven of our vision, and to whom our whole gushing soul goes forth, as if there were scarcely another being in the Universe; and as in that hour of love we feel the hands which are laid around our sinking souls to be the pierced hands, and the heart that throbs to ours the broken heart; so all along our Christian course, it is the same holy fascination which will not let us take our eyes from the awful lovely sight, of our Divine Friend and Elder Brother " bruised for our iniquities." And then in another solemn hour if the dying

saint has any image floating before his inward eye, when the last murmur has
ceased to attendant friends, and when the
glassy balls convey no light — it is the
image of *Christ on the Cross:* and when
(the next moment) the refreshed, healed,
and ransomed soul, is admitted to the vision of the Redeemer, it beholds him as
a "Lamb slain from the foundation of
the world." Christ will not have this
forgotten, even in the day of his victorious entry, to receive his spotless bride.
Though he who sitteth on the white horse
is the Faithful and True (v. 11) — the
King of kings and Lord of lords (v. 16)
— yea the very Word of God (v. 13) —
yet is he "clothed with a vesture dipped
in blood." Do not think my beloved
brethren, that there will be one saint in
glory, who will not feel that all pardon
safety and joy, and all there is in heaven,
have been purchased by the Lord Jesus
Christ in his priestly character. This it is
which pierces the heart of Christ's redeemed bride, that Christ should have died for
her. She can never forget it, in earth or
heaven. By this name, JESUS, the name

which tells of death, she would ever name her Lord: in these colours of crimson would she ever behold him. Deserving as He is of all robes of majesty and crowns of honour, none of them would so gloriously become his divine beauty and kingship, if he were not "clothed with a vesture dipped in blood." The breathing of his heart-broken church and turtle dove has continually been the same as of the individual penitent.

> "His dying crimson, like a robe
> Spreads o'er his body on the tree
> Then am I dead to all the globe
> And all the globe is dead to me."

5. But the power and majesty of Christ are to be shown, not merely over those who believe in him, that is to say, his Church, but over the world. The whole tenor of prophecy shows that there is a day coming when the Lord Jesus shall appear in his royalty, and when he shall have amends for all he has endured from his enemies. Our earth is waiting for a scene of glorious indemnity and reprisals. Say not that since the resurrection Christ

has suffered and been persecuted no more.
He hath suffered! With vastly more significancy than his servant Paul, can he say,
"Who is offended, and I burn not?" To
that same apostle, when yet a foe, he cried
from heaven, in terms that show how truly
he takes to himself all that is aimed at
his people, "Saul Saul why persecutest thou
me?" From his judgment throne he shall
say, "Inasmuch as ye did it not to the
least of these my brethren, ye did it not
to me." For centuries Christ's church has
been the mark for enemies; and as if
impatient at delay, "the souls of them that
were slain for the word of God, and for
the testimony which they held," have been
crying from beneath the altar, Rev. 6:9
"How long, O Lord, holy and true, dost
thou not judge and avenge our blood on
them that dwell on the earth?" Let no
careless sinner, let no froward opposer, persuade himself, that because our king Messiah is infinite in goodness, he is therefore
to do nothing in the universe but bless
and save. For such mistakers, it will be
too late, when the voice shall be heard
saying, Is. 63:4 "For the day of vengeance

is in my heart and the year of my redeemed is come." There is a day of vengeance; and to this some refer the vesture dipped in blood; finding a parallel in the words of Isaiah; "I have trodden the winepress alone, and of the people there was none with me; for I will tread them in mine anger, and trample them in my fury; and their blood shall be sprinkled upon my garments, and I will stain all my raiment." These words of Isaiah undeniably refer to the punishment which Christ shall inflict on his obstinate enemies. And our present context by no means excludes this idea of vindicatory justice; for see in v. 15. "Out of his mouth goeth a sharp sword, that with it he should smite the nations: and he shall rule them with a rod of iron, and he treadeth the winepress of the fierceness and wrath of Almighty God." The idea of Christ's vengeance, I say, is by no means excluded; and nevertheless I adhere to that common view of the text, which understands it as relating to sacrificial blood. He who rides in triumph appears primarily as God the Saviour, then as God the Judge. He is humbled before he is exalted. The propitiation and passion are the foundation of the triumph and the reign. Yet when the once-crucified Jesus re-appears and the armies which are in heaven follow him upon white horses, clothed in fine linen, white and clean,— the very love which he bears his church will cause him to destroy her oppressors. Age after age despots in church and state have forgotten it; yet as far back as the second psalm, v. 9 we remember to have heard it sung, unto Messiah, "Thou shalt break them with a rod of iron; thou shalt dash them in pieces like a potter's vessel." Again (Ps. 89:23) "I will beat down his foes before his face, and plague them that hate him." Nay it is a rule and a vindication, secured not only to our king, but to his church; for, if words have any meaning, we so read, (2:26) in the message to Thyatira: "And to him that overcometh, will I give power over the nations." So Paul comforts his Thessalonians (1:7) —"And to you who are troubled rest— with us—when the Lord Jesus shall be revealed from heaven with his mighty angels, in flaming fire taking vengeance on

them that know not God, and that obey
not the gospel of our Lord Jesus Christ."
How different this from what some expect
at Christ's appearing! He shall come not
only to give "rest," but to "take vengeance." And under this general head of
judicial recompense we can scarcely fail to
include Christ's *providential dealings with
kings and commonwealths.* Christ is king
of kings and king of commonwealths. All
the constitutions good and bad of the
world are unwittingly working out a prob-
lem which he hath set them. And sometimes when I hear of wars and convul-
sions and dethronements, it seems to me
that I am listening to the sound of earth-
en vessels, dashing one another to pieces,
in the violent rushing torrent of divine
destiny. He that died on Calvary holds a
guiding hand over all the changes of mankind. In the scroll of prophecy some parts
are but half-unrolled, as yet. Still, amidst
much darkness there are some things which
we can read, in characters of flame. All
the future is not to be days of peace.
Whatever the advocates of perfectibilian progress may say, and whatever dreams they

may have of a golden age and Saturnian
kingdoms, when they shall have destroyed
property and marriage and the sabbath
and the church — he that sitteth in the
heavens shall laugh, the Lord shall have
them in derision; "Then shall he speak
unto them in his sore displeasure." These
retributions are yet in reserve. Ever since
our Lord rode in triumph over prostrate
Jerusalem, he has from time to time been
making bare his arm in behalf of his
church. The eye of the student of prophecy sees one grand retribution, as vivid as
lightning. BABYLON awaits her destruction.
If the volcanic fires that break out sometimes at Etna and sometimes at Vesuvius,
and smoulder under the whole Campagna,
were all at once to unsettle the seven
hills, and physically shake down the seat
of antichristian tyranny, the explosion would
not be more sudden nor the overthrow
more complete, than that which we expect
for Babylon. No abridgment can be made
of the eighteenth chapter—we see her glory—we see her fall—we behold the com-
mercial nations standing afar off and be-
wailing her desolation: v. 20 "Rejoice over

her, thou heavens and ye holy apostles and prophets; for God hath avenged you on her." The hour is at hand, my brethren, when to be on Christ's side will be the only safety in the universe; when his enemies shall in the sight of all intelligent beings, be confounded; and when those that "love his appearing" shall shine forth like the sun.

6. More particularly, the exaltation of our atoning Lord is connected with the variety and greatness of his realms: "On his head were many crowns." It is not a single sovereignty. Many crowns import diversity of rule and empire. He is "King of kings and Lord of lords," and rightfully bears the diadems of all the kings and lords over whom he reigns. He that was slain, has by virtue of his death, the crown of the church; he wears it, benignant in love, the royal bridegroom, who can never for a moment forget the crown of thorns, which he wore for her sake. He has the crown of the nations; "the kingdoms of this world are become the kingdom of our Lord and of his Christ." As the day approaches we may expect the wheels to run

round more rapidly; more thrones will totter; more dynasties will crumble away, and fall into the political crater; more oppressions will cease; more brotherhoods will coalesce; more commerce will knit together continents; more discoveries will harmonize conflicting interests; more liberty will be granted to religion; more ships will be freighted with the word; more kings shall be nursing fathers and queens nursing mothers, until the day when "he who blesseth himself in the earth shall bless himself in the God of truth, and he that sweareth in the earth shall swear by the God of truth: because the former troubles are forgotten, and because they are hid from mine eyes." More visibly shall Jesus then reign over the nations. He has farther the crown of the Universe; and he has it because of his bloodshedding and death. He who (in the text) says "his name is called the Word of God" is the same apostle who elsewhere ascribes to that mysterious name the creation of the world. "He was in the world, and the world was made by him, and the world knew him not." Had they known him, they would not have crucified the Lord of glory. But on that very cross he triumphed over them, and his many crowns well comport with the vesture dipped in blood. He died — "wherefore God also hath highly exalted him, and given him a name which is above every name; that at the name of Jesus every knee should bow, of things in heaven and things in earth and things under the earth." "All things were created Col. 1:16 by him and for him; and he is before all things, and by him all things consist." There is no higher name, there is no more regal glory. When we arrive in our ascent at Christ Jesus, we reach the acme of divine sovereignty; we are brought to rest in the centre. And this illustrates and magnifies the condescending grace and compassion whereby such creatures (as we have been) are allowed to approach the infinite Ruler. Is it credible, that God the Word, incarnate, should have purchased such an exaltation—for such sinners—and by such means? by dying, for them, the accursed death of the cross! Is it credible? Yea, faith receives it; as the prime doctrine of religion. Here is the down-

ward flight of pity and love, which no
comprehension of mind can measure. . . .
God *so* loved the world! He has a right
to reign; first over us, then over all. Let
the circle widen, from self, and family, and
acquaintanceship, and state, and country,
and language, and church, and planet, and
system, till the universe be taken into the
sweep of his dominion, and all worlds con-
tribute to his many crowns! Each humbled, panting soul will say, Lord whatever
men, and whatever worlds may reject thee
—thou shalt reign over ME! *Here*, HERE
is thy throne. Forgive me, forgive me, O
forgive me—that I have been so long withholding this homage! Forgive me, incarnate Love, that other lords beside thee
have had dominion over me. Take the
full overflowing tide of all my affections,
O Jesus! Would God the vessel were
more capacious! Would God, that millions
of other hearts might join, to make the
sacrifice of praise more worthy. O thou
who · art clothed in a vesture dipped in
blood, in this land of my exile and home-
sickness I will anticipate the song of glory, and say, These crowns become thee!

Rule thou in the midst of thine enemies! for thou art worthy!

7. Such are the contrasts afforded by this wonderful glimpse of coming day: we are carried directly from the cross to the throne. And this occasions no shock to the loving mind; for as there never was a true believer who did not grieve with Christ in his sufferings, as if the soul itself had been in part the guilty cause of this suffering,—so, I suppose, there never was a true believer who did not rejoice with Christ in his heavenly recompense and exaltation. Who that knows the Lord does not exult to think that every conceivable diadem of glory is put upon his head; and that he is coming to be acknowledged by the universe as King of kings and Lord of lords? Yes Christians—ye shall be among the multitude, whose utterance, "as the voice of many waters and as the voice of mighty thunderings, shall be, "Alleluia: for the Lord God omnipotent reigneth!"

O my brethren, and ye who sit here so unconcerned, these are solemn times, which are coming upon the earth! None of that news from beyond sea, which so

much excites you, is to be compared to
these certain changes! The sublunary revo-
lutions are only precursors of the grand,
divine revolution. You are perhaps nearer
to the point of observation, than you are
willing to think. Presently, who knows but
you shall hear a "great voice from heaven,
saying *Come up hither!*" Whether you
live long enough on earth, to witness any
indubitable signs of Christ's coming, or not,
you will very soon be called to judgment,
and will taste the experience of heaven or
hell. How will your scorching eyeballs
shrink back into their orbits, from before
him whose eyes are as a flame of fire—if
you shall have been finally impenitent!
Of what profit will it be to you to have
seen unfolded so often this vesture dipped
in blood; so often to have turned your
back on Sacraments; so often to have
been directed and invited and besought to
take part in this propitiation; if then, after
all, you shall behold in Jesus Christ, not
a pardoning God, but an avenging Judge?
Of what profit will it be to you, to behold Christ arrayed in majesty and crowned
with dominion, and followed by the armies

16

of heaven, if, at the dread moment, conscience shall rise and tell you, that your portion is henceforth with the fearful, the abominable, and the unbelieving! But why need it so be? Behold the lamb of God, that taketh away the sin of the world! The spot from which I address you seems bedewed with the blood of Christ. Every thing Sacramental is full of invitation. Though you may have entered those doors in utter carelessness, why should you not now be subdued by the mighty argument of the Cross? Your inexcusable delay does but magnify your danger. You cannot be sure of another offer of Christ as long as you live. "To-day, if ye will hear his voice, harden not your hearts!"

And you, my beloved Christian brethren who have come with me to surround the table of the Lord; you who know him; you who have tasted that the Lord is gracious; you who have with the full concert of every power of soul, humbly but delightedly given yourselves away to Christ, and who would gladly renew the gift a thousand thousand times, adding to it if you could the inhabitants of a thousand

thousand worlds; you come hither this day
with a welcome! Of this you need have
no doubt. Let me for your encouragement
dwell in conclusion on two thoughts. (1)
You are coming to one who is clothed in
a vesture dipped in blood. You are coming
to him who died for you (the simplest but
greatest truth in all religion). Here on this
table, you will behold the broken body and
shed blood of the Lord Jesus. If now this
Redeemer lays such stress on his sacrificial
work and precious bloodshedding, as not
even to ride in triumph without the badge
of his death, how confidently may you approach the eucharistic table with hope of
being received! The very intention of the
rite is to show forth that very death, which
is the sole foundation of a sinner's life.
The day is coming, I know, when Christ is
to be on a throne of judgment. THEN having died in your sins it will indeed be too
late to pray to him; and though you pray
to rocks and mountains, they will no more
melt, at your cry, than your hearts have
melted at the cry of God. But now, Jesus
is upon the throne of grace. He treats
with you from the mercy-seat. It is a

duty you owe him, to cast away these unbelieving hesitations. He commands you to
believe; He commands you to rejoice. He
offers you himself, as gratuitously as we
offer you this bread and wine. And still
I think I perceive some of you, even of
long standing in Christianity, murmuring in
your tents as if it were false that "this
man receiveth sinners." You doubt and
distrust. This has come upon you for your
sins, your worldly compliances, your neglects, your idolatries. You have lost your
evidences, and are afraid of your Saviour.
—But O tell me, is this the way to treat
one who died for you! Shame on your
scruples and delay; Come boldly to the
throne of grace, and to the table of mercy,
that you may obtain mercy and find grace
to help in time of need. For (2) you
are coming to one, who bears on his head
many crowns. You are coming to a King.
Therefore enlarge your petitions. Be not
niggardly in your expectations, as though
these gifts went by desert. It is the very
first thing which you have to unlearn in
religion. The promise is, "I am he who
brought thee out of the land of Egypt;

open thy mouth wide and I will fill it."
I am he that redeemed thee—make large
requests, and be satisfied. This Great King
has invited you here to bless you. He is
able to subdue your enemies and deliver
you from your sins. You cannot ask too
much of spiritual good for your soul. You
cannot ask more than Christ's death has
merited. You cannot ask more than Christ's
power can effect. You are at liberty to
multiply your prayers, in the way of intercession, for those whom you bring in the
love of your hearts, to this sacred place.
Where are you? Is not this a King's
court? Is not the master of the Assembly
King of kings and Lord of lords? Be in
haste to include in your petition all whom
you would look around for, if the next
moment should bring the crash of the
Universe. Can you ascend to heaven without these souls! Can you clasp to your bosom one whom you may yet see at Christ's
left hand! Go further—stretch more wide
the arms of comprehensive benevolence!
Take in a world of sinners. You are in
the presence-chamber of that King, who
cried "And I, if I be lifted up from the

earth, will draw all men unto me."—By all his atoning blood, by all his regal crowns, plead with him, instantly, and importunately, that he would speedily come and turn his enemies into friends! All the other thoughts, desires and passions of life ought to be swallowed up in this, and would be . . . . if we only saw things aright. No object, conceivable by man, can stand comparison for an instant with the reign of Christ over a subdued world. Perish all gain, all power, all science, all art, all honor, in comparison. Let the same mind be in you, that was in Christ Jesus. Look out for the deepest, fathomless part of the ocean, for a place whereinto to cast forever that burdensome millstone about your neck . . . I mean *Self!* Show it no mercy! For Christ—for his Cross—for his Crown— for his people—count all things but loss.